GARDENING
IN
THE MIDDLE EAST

Merry Christmas
With love
Hamed, Farah &
Jessica xxx
'89

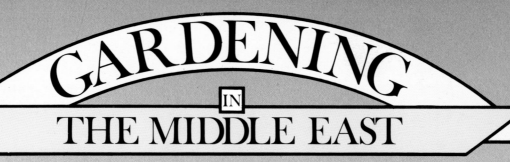

GARDENING
IN
THE MIDDLE EAST

ERIC MOORE

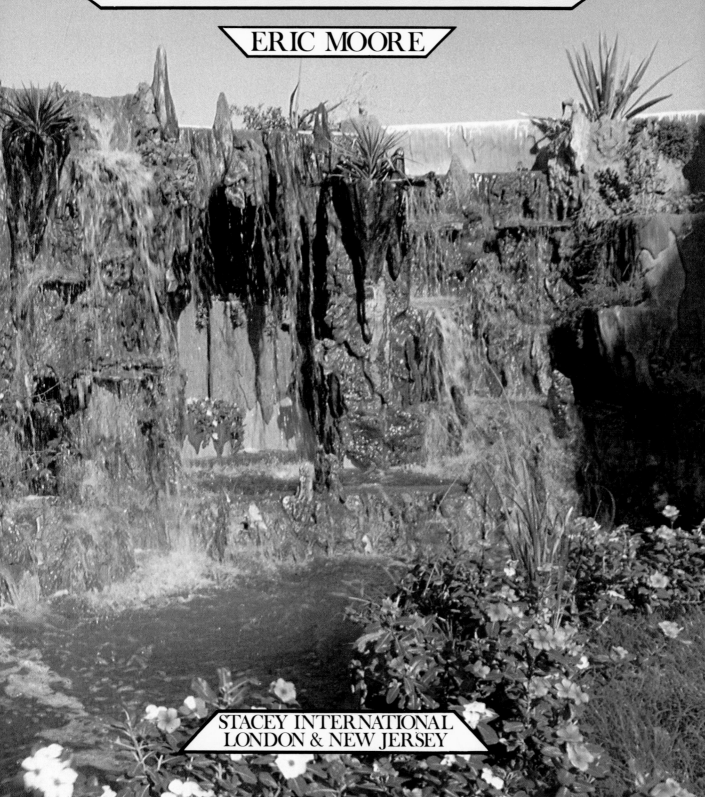

STACEY INTERNATIONAL
LONDON & NEW JERSEY

Editorial
John Blackett-Ord
Kitty Carruthers

Design
Keith Savage
David Cringle

Index
Martyn Gilchrist

Gardening in the Middle East

First published by Stacey International 1986
128 Kensington Church Street, London W8 4BH
Telex 298768 STACEY G

Set in Linotronic Baskerville by
SX Composing Ltd, Essex, England

Manufactured by
Regent Publishing Services Ltd

Printed and bound in Hong Kong by
Leefung-Asco Printers Ltd

British Library Cataloguing-in-Publication Data

Moore, Eric
    Gardening in the Middle East
    1. Gardening — Near East
    I. Title
    635′.0956   SB453.3.N2

    ISBN 0-905743-49-0

Library of Congress Cataloging-in-Publication
Data

Moore, Eric.
    Gardening in the Middle East.

    Bibliography: p.
    Includes index.
    1. Gardening – Near East. 2. Desert gardening –
Near East. I. Title.
SB453.3.N23M66 1986   635.9′51′56   86-22959
ISBN 0-905473-49-0

CONTENTS

ACKNOWLEDGEMENTS

My deep thanks go to Isaak Diqqs, BADAN Co, Riyadh, and Morgan Holt, Venturesearch Inc, Phoenix, Arizona, USA, for reviewing the accuracy of my efforts; to the Riyadh staff of Ciba-Geigy Saudi Arabia Ltd for their generous help and suggestions; and to Professor Wilhelm Buttiker of the Meteorological and Environmental Protection Administration, Jeddah, for his assistance on climatic information.

I am also grateful to Symonds-Tramor for allowing me flexibility in my work schedule, but, most importantly, gratitude goes to my wife Deanne for her encouragement and faith.

INTRODUCTION

THE PURPOSE of this book is to help you make your own garden in the harsh environment of searing heat and dehydrating winds that prevails over so much of the Middle East.

At first sight, it may seem surprising that plants can flourish in such conditions and in a medium so seemingly arid as the sand and highly alkaline limestone that covers most of the Arabian peninsula and many other regions in the Middle East. But with care and selectivity in the soil preparation and in the choice of plants, beautiful, lush and colourful gardens can be created and maintained. And each year, happily, increasing evidence of this can be found in the streets and suburbs of Egypt and of Jordan, of Saudi Arabia, Oman and the Gulf States.

Traditionally, of course, gardens have always occupied a central position in Middle Eastern life. After all, the original among gardens – the Garden of Eden – bloomed here, even though its precise location (in Bahrain perhaps, or Yemen, or in the Asir region of Saudi Arabia) remains open to interpretation.

And the desert garden, the oasis, played a vital role in trade and travel, its cool waters refreshing the weary travellers and their camels. But water was not the only benefit oases provided. The cool shade of the date palms and the lush green of the *berseem* (alfalfa) or vegetables growing beneath them created a peaceful garden setting that offered beauty and tranquillity to the Bedouin. Many of these groves can be seen today much the same as they were hundreds of years ago. The 'garden city' of Najran in Saudi Arabia typifies this combination of natural beauty and food production.

But for all of Islam, the ultimate garden is the reward that follows a life of practising the seven pillars of wisdom – Paradise. The Quran tells us this is Allah's garden of spreading shade, streams, fountains, and cool pavilions.

In writing this book I have presumed no existing gardening knowledge on the part of the reader. It is intended as much for the amateur gardener who wants to create his or her own patch of greenery, however simple or ambitious – from a box of herbs to a precisely planned formal garden – as for the professional landscape gardener employed on municipal or private projects.

Seven separate climatic zones within the Middle East have been identified and delineated on the map on pp. 10-11, and the zones in which each plant can be cultivated successfully are listed under its entry in the plant encyclopedia (see pp. 77-137).

In this way it is hoped that the book can be of precise practical value to the reader, wherever they may be gardening in the Middle East, be it in the arid desert interiors of Egypt, Eastern Jordan or Saudi Arabia, in the humid coastal environment of Jeddah or Muscat or any of the Emirates, or perhaps high in the mountains of Saudi Arabia's Asir region or the Musandam in Oman.

Wherever you may be gardening, the rewards can be many and varied. And whether you are brightening up a corner or making a compound home your own; beautifying a swimming pool or recreating a formal garden from memory, there is always that sense of real accomplishment that only growing plants can give.

May Allah smile with kindness on your efforts.

Eric Moore, 1986

HOW TO USE THIS BOOK

THE BOOK is divided into four parts. The first three parts tackle the kind of major, practical questions that anyone who is gardening in the Middle East must ask themselves at the outset.

- What sort of garden do I want?
- What plants are best-suited to such a garden?
- What climatic and soil conditions do I have to contend with?
- How do I grow such plants in such conditions?

The task of picking the right plant for the purpose and location you have in mind has been simplified by drawing together into tables many of the alternatives available and listing them by different categories such as growth habit (eg shrubs, vines and ground covers), function (eg shade trees, hedges), flower duration and fragrance.

This allows the reader to take in the options at a glance, make a comparison and select the appropriate plant for the job, a process which a straightforward, alphabetical plant encyclopedia (useful though this is) does not enable you to do.

Sections on every aspect of plant cultivation – soil mixes, planting, watering, fertilizing, pruning, propagation, pest and disease control – complete this comprehensive introduction to Middle Eastern gardening.

The fourth part, the plant encyclopedia (pp. 77-137) provides a detailed, alphabetical listing of nearly 350 plants of every type that can successfully be grown in the Middle East. Details of botanical classification, height and size, leaf, flower and fruit shape, colour and flowering seasons, are given under each entry, together with the salient points on the cultivation of the plant, such as pruning, watering, propagation and control of pests and diseases.

The climatic zones in which it should be possible to cultivate each plant are identified under its entry.

CLIMATIC ZONES IN THE MIDDLE EAST

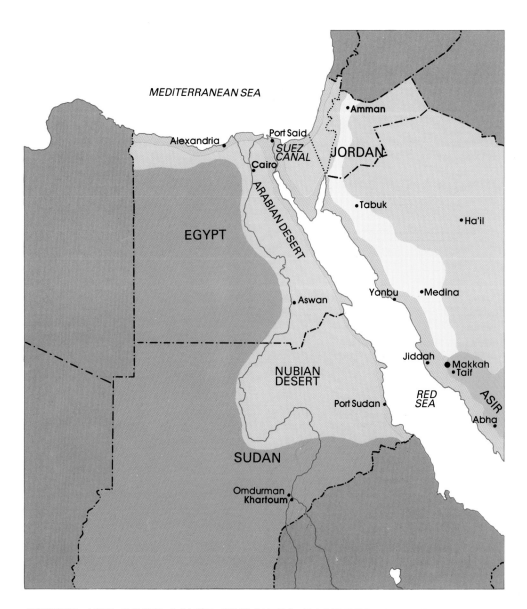

THERE ARE FOUR MAIN CLIMATIC FACTORS that affect a plant's survival: temperature, humidity, wind, and rainfall. The Middle East offers a broad weather spectrum, from the snows of Saudi Arabia's Asir Province to the overpowering humidity of the Gulf and from the searing heat of the Rub Al Khali to the monsoon rains of the Qara mountains in Oman's Dhofar region.

For the purposes of this book, the area can be roughly divided into seven separate types of climatic zones. Some of the hardier plant species will grow in all of them, others in only two or three. The map shows the borders and locations of these zones, but these of necessity can only be approximations. There may be areas or 'pockets' in each zone which take on the characteristics of another zone.

The climatic factors that determine these zones can be defined as follows:

Zone 1: The humid African and Arabian coastal areas of the Red Sea, extending to the nearby foothills. In Egypt this zone extends up to the Mediterranean coast,

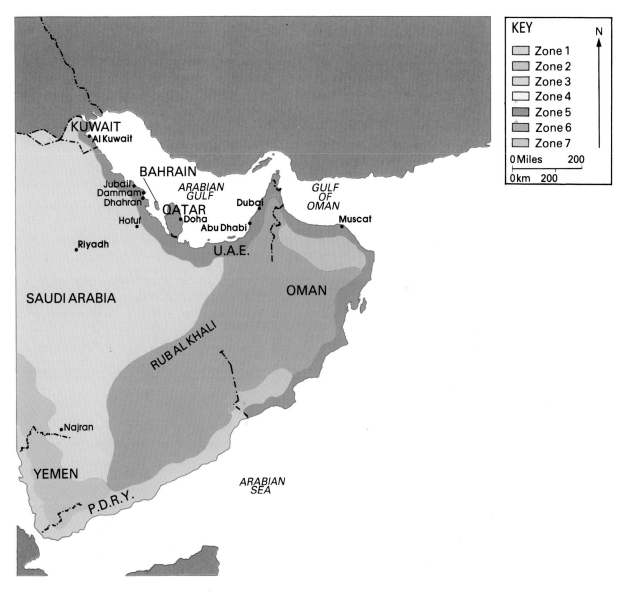

including the Nile delta, and west to the Libyan border.

   Average high temperatures: 40° to 45°C (104° to 113°F)

   Average low temperatures: 11° to 15°C (52° to 59°F)

   Average humidity: 80% (winter), 92% (summer)

   Average annual rainfall: 45mm to 64mm (2 to 2.5in)

Zone 2: The mountains and higher elevations of Saudi Arabia's south-western Asir Province and Oman's Akhdar mountains. Characterised by heavy annual rainfall influenced by monsoon winds, and winter temperatures below freezing.

   Average high temperatures: 32° to 38°C (90° to 100°F)

   Average low temperatures: 0° to −5°C (32° to 23°F)

   Average humidity: 40% to 60%

   Average annual rainfall: 160mm (6in) in Taif; 564mm (22.5in) in Jabal Salah, Saudi Arabia

11

Zone 3: The arid central and north central regions of the Arabian peninsula extending up to the eastern areas of Jordan. Also includes the regions of Egypt and north Sudan from the Red Sea foothills to the Nile. Elevations from 150m to 1,000m (500-3,000ft). Mild winters and occasional frost, and hot, dry summers with moderate to heavy winds.

    Average high temperatures: 41° to 46°C (106° to 115°F)
    Average low temperatures: 8° to 2°C (46° to 36°F)
    Average humidiy: 45% (winter), 18% (summer)
    Average annual rainfall: 35mm to 100mm (1.5 to 4in)

Zone 4: Semi-arid northern and north-western higher elevations, including the populous areas of Jordan. Not as cold as Saudi Arabia's Asir Province, and nowhere near the same level of rainfall. Although the average rainfall is comparable to the central areas, the extended period of frost and higher humidity make this a distinct zone.

    Average high temperatures: 30° to 41°C (86° to 106°F)
    Average low temperatures: 2° to −7°C (36° to 10°F)
    Average humidiy: 35% to 55%
    Average annual rainfall: 78mm to 120mm (3 to 5 in)

Zone 5: The humid coastal area of the Arabian Gulf, from Kuwait to the straits of Hormuz, including Bahrain and Qatar, then south and west along the Omani coast.

    Average high temperatures: 42° to 47°C (108° to 117°F)
    Average low temperatures: 13° to 10° (56° to 50°F)
    Average humidity: 75% (winter), 90% (summer)
    Average annual rainfall: 50mm to 100mm (2 to 4 in)

Zone 6: The harsh desert areas of the Sahara and Saudi Arabia's Rub Al Khali, which have very high summer temperatures, cold winter nights, and harsh winds. These regions are estimated to have the lowest rainfall in the Middle East. Some areas may not have rain for years.

    Average high temperatures: 42° to 47°C (108° to 117°F)
    Average low temperatures: 7° to 1°C (45° to 34°F)
    Average humidity: 40% (winter), 15% (summer)
    Average annual rainfall: 20mm to 40mm (1 to 2 in)

Zone 7: The Qara mountains in south-western Oman which experience heavy monsoon rains blowing off the Indian Ocean from June to September. The mountains are the natural barrier that prevents these summer rains from reaching southern Saudi Arabia and the Red Sea coast of Africa.

    Average high temperatures: 26° to 32°C (79° to 90°F)
    Average low temperatures: 2° to −4°C (36° to 25°F)
    Average humidity: 40% to 80%
    Average annual rainfall: 250mm to 625mm (10 to 25 in)

The above figures are approximate averages, and are based on data obtained from Saudi Arabia's Meteorological and Environmental Protection Administration.

SECTION ONE
TYPES OF GARDENS FOUND IN THE MIDDLE EAST

TRADITIONAL ISLAMIC GARDENS

A modern
treatment of the old
tradition

THE DESIGNS AND SYMMETRY of traditional Islamic gardens are rooted in the deep religious tenets of Islam and the culture of the Arab people. They are gardens of hospitality and privacy. They are inward-directed, focusing beauty on the interior rather than the exterior. Walls that are drab and undecorated on the outside may enclose a delightfully lush, shaded garden on the inside. Where European gardens are designed for walking and strolling, these are for people who are sitting and at rest. They are gardens with order, balance, and geometric design, usually divided into four equal parts, with walkways between, and a central single jet fountain or small reflection pool in the centre with narrow channels leading into it. They are typified by the magnificent Alhambra in Granada, Spain.

Islamic gardens are designed to achieve harmony and peace. They provide shade and relief from the sun's glare and heat. Frequently they take the form of a courtyard with massed plantings, employing repeated patterns to complement the 'hardscape' patterns in walls and walkways, sometimes with a central pavilion. An ornate entry gate serves as a focal point and a welcoming area.

FORMAL GARDENS

FORMAL GARDENS bring to mind the grand, intricate, geometrically designed royal European gardens of centuries past, such as Versailles in France or Hampton Court in England. They are characterized by straight lines, rectangular shapes, and carefully clipped hedges. Such gardens are evenly balanced and symmetrical. Walkways are straight and paved, instead of curving gravel paths or stepping stones. Low, even borders are favoured, using one variety of plant rather than a mixture of foliage, height, and colours. Lawns are smooth, level, and manicured. The beauty is in the order and symmetry. If water is present, it is so as a long, narrow reflecting pool, perhaps, or a marble fountain, rather than a natural stone waterfall. Some such gardens include topiary, with privet or myrtle or yew pruned and clipped into exotic shapes or animals.

Many of the plants used in the great European gardens will not grow in the more arid climate of the Middle East but there are a number of plants that can be shaped to produce the formal effect. Trees like *Ficus nitida* and olive can be pruned to cube or globe shapes. Clerodendron, dodonea, lantana, and even oleander can be clipped into a rectangular hedge or a myriad of topiary shapes. Contrasting, even borders can be created using the grey foliage of *Senecio cineraria* (Dusty Miller) or santolina.

Careful and detailed planning, particularly in the selection of plant varieties, is the critical factor in creating a successful formal garden. Frequent and skilled maintenance is an absolute necessity. Generally, a garden design is more effective if the two design concepts, 'free form' and 'formal' are not mixed. The attempt to combine the characteristics of each tends to dilute the dramatic effects that can be achieved by each type of design.

Formal concepts in a Middle Eastern park

FREE FORM OR NATURAL GARDENS

Lawn of Bermuda Grass with (left) *Eucalyptus rudis* (Desert Gum) and *Parkinsonia aculeta* (Jerusalem Thorn)

FREE FORM GARDENS attempt to reproduce the grand scope of nature, but within the limitations of a confined space. Here we see curved and free-flowing lines as opposed to straight and rectangular; asymmetrical shapes and spaces, as opposed to balance and order.

This type of design can include mounded and rolling shapes of grass areas with boulder groupings or tufts of annual flowers. Curving gravel walkways with random drifts of various ground covers flanked by tree groupings may try to convey the feel of a meandering meadow or forest footpath. Screening trees or shrubs can be placed at the garden perimeter, or vines against the surrounding wall. There may be an assortment of shrubs placed in a planned, but seemingly random, pattern throughout a ground cover area, with the smaller shrubs in the foreground. If water effects are to be used, a natural stone waterfall and small wandering stream, powered by a simple recirculating pump, is effective. Trees of varying heights, spread, foliage, and flower colour help to give an uncontrived, natural feel to the landscape. A pergola of natural wood or local adobe (mud) with a palm frond roof can add to the effect.

There are other details that help to achieve this theme: thin, curving wood header boards, used to separate gravel paths from grass or ground cover areas; trailing plants such as *Asparagus sprengeri* or *Lantana montividensis* that cascade over low walls; large individual boulders or rock groupings sprinkled throughout ground covers and at the base of walls; natural stone stepping stones instead of concrete walks.

NATIVE DESERT GARDENS

IN NATIVE DESERT GARDENS the purpose is to recreate, on a smaller scale, the stark, dry, rocky landscape of the escarpments and canyons that border the actual desert. Large boulders, sometimes one on top of the other, rock-strewn bare ground, random native plants, and small wadis typify this effect. A superb example of this is the nature walk and man-made berms around the perimeter of the Diplomatic Quarter in Riyadh, in Saudi Arabia.

A native desert garden

To achieve this effect dramatically in a home garden is a difficult logistical problem. The large boulders, sometimes weighing up to one-and-a-half tons, need to be transported and carefully positioned. To carry out the theme effectively, native desert plants should be used, and these are almost impossible to find in local nurseries. One reason for this is that many desert varieties, evolved in the harsh arid environment, are thorny, small-leafed, and somewhat unattractive. Seed can be gathered by hand from plants in the desert or wadis, but this requires almost year-round effort and many hours of hiking. Also, if trees are started from seed, it may be years before they are large enough to make a significant statement in the garden. Substitute plants from nursery stock can be used, but it takes an experienced eye to select those that will give the natural effect.

In this book we have listed only a few of the more commonly used natives, as there are other books available dealing specifically with wildflowers and indigenous plants. However, if your mind is made up to take the challenge, here are some varieties that could be used: **Trees:** *Acacia arabica, Prosopis spicigera, Ficus pseudosycamoris.* **Shrubs, Ground covers, Flowers:** *Atriplex, Calotropis, Clitoria, Datura, Diplotaxus, Okradensis, Pennisetum, Periclopa, Teucrium.*

FOOD PRODUCING GARDENS

Hand pollination of
a female date palm

IN THE EARLY HISTORY of the Middle East, it was imperative that every garden should have a food-producing function. As it still is, underground water was finite and annual rainfall meagre. Today, the date palm groves are amongst the most inviting garden settings, often with a *berseem* (alfalfa) or vegetable crop growing beneath them.

In a private garden, nutritional plants can take up the entire plot, occupy a small corner, or just provide an individual focal point, such as a citrus tree.

Different types of food-producing gardens are listed on the following pages:

Home-grown herbs and spices add freshness and flavour to your cooking

HERB GARDENS

A wide variety of herbs and spices can be grown in the Middle East. They are popular not only for their flavours, but also because they provide an attractive assortment of shapes, sizes, colours and scents. The most desirable situation for your herbs is the one in which they will have full sun most of the year, but are shaded from June-August. For a small area, this can be accomplished by stretching cloth over them for shade in the hotter months. They can be grown in pots or planter boxes scattered in strategic places around a patio, or can be integrated into the landscape. Some can be clipped as formal hedges, others as shrubs or borders, and some make a fragrant green carpet. Grey foliage plants make a good contrast. Most are grown from seed.

Listed below are herbs categorized by landscape situations and/or by use. Each one is also described in the plant encyclopedia (see pp. 77-137).

Cooking herbs: basil (*Ocimum*), caraway (*Carum*), chives (*Allium*), coriander (*Coriandrum*), dill (*Anethum*), sweet marjoram (*Majorana*), mint (*Mentha*), oregano (*Origanum*), parsley (*Petroselinum crispum*), rosemary (*Rosmarinum*), sage (*Salvia*), savory (*Satureja*), tarragon (*Artemesia*), thyme (*Thymus*).
Ground covers: rosemary, various thymes, chamomile (*Anthemis*).
Shrubs: anise (*Pimpinella*), lavander (*Lavendula*), wormwood (*Artemesia*).
Formal clipped hedges: germander (*Teucrium*), santolina.
Borders: basil, mint, parsley, sage, savory, tarragon.
Grey foliage: germander, lavender, sage, wormwood.

DRYING HERBS FOR COOKING:

Leafy herbs These are ready to cut when the flower buds start to form, and full flavour is obtained up until the flowers are half open. Cut early in the day before the sun gets too hot, but after the dew has dried on the leaves. This is when the oil (flavour) content is at its highest. Perennial herbs should not be cut back for drying more than one third at each cutting, annual herbs no lower than 10-12cm (4-5in) from the ground. You will generally get two to three crops during the summer, but do not cut perennial herbs after October.

Before drying, remove dead or insect-damaged leaves, and sort out any weeds. Wash off dust and dirt in cool water, then shake off excess moisture. To dry small-leafed herbs such as rosemary or thyme, tie them in small bundles and hang them upside down from a line stretched across a dark room or closet. The room must be warm and have good air circulation to aid rapid drying and the retention of the flavouring aromatic oils. For large-leafed herbs such as basil, remove leaves from branches and spread over a perforated tray or screen with two layers of cheese cloth between the tray surface and the leaves. Stir leaves daily.

If the above procedures are followed, the leafy herbs should be dry enough to crumble in 3-8 days. Remove leaves from stems and store whole in airtight glass or ceramic containers. To retain the maximum flavour, wait until you are using them in cooking, then crumble the leaves and mix them into the food. Check the jars the first few days to be sure no moisture is forming. If it does, pour out the leaves, and dry them for a few days more. Label each jar with the name of the herb and date filled.

Seed herbs In plants such as anise, caraway, and dill, the flavouring is found in the seeds. Collect the seed clusters when the seeds turn brown and start to fall off if shaken gently. Leave a little stem when you cut the clusters, then shake, and spread the seeds out in the sun to dry for a few days. Then separate the chaff from the seed, and continue to dry in the sun for two weeks. Store in jars as you did the leafy herbs.

A wide range of vegetables may be grown in the Middle East

VEGETABLES

An entire book could be written describing how to grow vegetables in the Middle East – but that is another book. Here we give a brief description of when to plant by zones, and a list of selected vegetables by season. The quality and taste of most vegetables is affected by saline water and alkaline soil, so, where possible, irrigate with water low in salts, and use a soil rich in organic material.

Cool-season vegetables

Cool-season vegetables produce their best growth before or after the peak summer temperatures. In zones 1, 3, 5 and 6 (see pp. 10-11), such vegetables should be planted from late January to early March so that they can be harvested before June 1st; alternatively plant in early September so that maximum growth occurs during the autumn, and the crop can be harvested from December to March. If you are in areas of zones 2, 4 and 7 where you should not experience heavy frost, cool-season vegetables can be planted all year round.

Cool-season vegetables include:

Artichoke	Celery	Peas
Asparagus	Garlic	Potato
Beet	Kale	Radish
Broccoli	Kohlrabi	Rhubarb
Brussel Sprouts	Leek	Shallots
Cabbage	Lettuce	Spinach
Carrots	Onion	Turnip
Cauliflower	Parsnip	

Warm weather vegetables

As their name suggests, warm weather vegetables experience their best growth, and produce their crops during high temperatures. However, in zones 1,3 and 5, the June-August heat in full sun may be too much for many varieties, and so it is wise to shade the plants during this time. Warm weather vegetables include:

Beans	Okra
Collards	Squash
Corn	Sweet Potato
Cucumber	Swiss Chard
Eggplant	Tomato
Melon	Zucchini

Some vegetable plants are also attractive enough to double as ornamentals in your garden. Grown as bedding plants, in borders, or in containers, they will add colour and interest. Some of these ornamental varieties are also perennials, so that they will brighten up your garden year after year. The ornamental vegetables include:

Artichoke (perennial)	Red Cabbage
Asparagus (perennial)	Rhubarb (perennial)
Kale	Swiss Chard

Citrus fruit trees, such as this orange, thrive in the Middle East

FOOD-PRODUCING TREES

Citrus
Citrus generally do well in the Middle East in all areas except the higher mountains and the desert. They make excellent landscape trees or large shrubs. Evergreen, they are adaptable to pruning as a standard tree, multi-trunk tree, or dense, rounded shrub. Use them as a focal point in a lawn, for screening against a wall, in a ground cover area, or use the dwarf varieties in containers. If space is available, a citrus grove composed of oranges, lemons, lime, grapefruit, and the various cross-hybrids, will give a garden a mediterranean look. For growing details and a list of varieties, see the plant encyclopedia section under Citrus.

Deciduous fruit trees
These include almond, apple, apricot, cherry, nectarine, peach, plum and prune. Most deciduous fruit trees require cold winters and frost, and they are generally only grown in areas where these requirements will be met. Their value as landscape trees in these areas is enhanced by the beautiful flowering in the spring and, with some plum varieties, the red to purple foliage from early spring to late autumn. For detailed descriptions, see the plant encyclopedia section under Fruit Trees, Deciduous.

Date palms
The date palm has of course provided the Middle East with a staple harvest for centuries, and needs no introduction. Details on growing and cultivating date palms are listed in the plant encyclopedia under *Phoenix dactylifera.*

SECTION TWO
HOW TO CHOOSE THE RIGHT PLANT

HOW TO CHOOSE THE RIGHT PLANT

(above) *Althea rosea* (Hollyhock), (above right) *Lantana camara*

PERHAPS the most difficult task in creating a pleasing garden or landscape is to select and identify the right plants to achieve the desired effect. Which trees are safest around a pool? Are there vines available with yellow flowers that will cover a wall? Are shrubs available that grow only 1 metre (3ft) tall? Are there suitable trees that lose their leaves (deciduous) in the winter if you want sun around a patio? This section of the book describes the uses to which different plants can be put and how they can be used in different settings. It differentiates between the myriad of sizes, shapes, colours, and textures that are available, and has been planned to help you solve your garden problems one by one. The Latin botanical names are used because in many cases these are the names you will need at a nursery to buy the plant. Where the common name differs from the Latin name, it also is shown. If there is a particular plant you want information on, and you only know the common English name, the plant encylopedia should have it listed with a cross reference to the botanical name.

SHADE TREES AND STREET TREES

LISTED BELOW are trees whose growth habit is such that they spread wide enough to produce significant shade. They have all been used in some of the major cities in the Middle East by municipal authorities as street trees lining sidewalks or forming road dividers. By using the pictures and the descriptions in the plant encyclopedia, a novice gardener should be able to identify each of the species, perhaps with a little help from the local nursery or garden shop.

Key:
d deciduous
e evergreen
a 3m to 5m (10ft to 17ft)
b 5m to 10m (17ft to 33ft)
c 10m (33ft) or larger
y flowers
n insignificant or no flowers

	type	climatic zones	height	spread	flowering
Acacia farnesiana (Sweet Acacia)	e	all	a	a	y
Albizzia lebbeck (Mother's Tongue)	d	all	b	b	y
Azederacha indica (Neem Tree)	e	1,5	b	b	n
Casuarina equisitifolia (Beefwood)	e	all	c	a	n
Ceratonia siliqua (Carob)	e	all	b	b	n
Conocarpus lancifolia (Button Mangrove)	e	1,3,5,7	b	b	y
Delonix regia (Royal Poinciana)	d	all but 6	c	c	y
Eucalyptus camaldulensis (Red Gum)	e	all	c	b	n
Eucalyptus sideroxylon (Pink Ironbark)	e	all	c	b	y
Ficus nitida (Indian Laurel)	e	1,3,4,5,7	b	b	n
Jacaranda acutifolia (Jacaranda)	d	all but 6	b	b	y
Melia azederach (China Berry)	d	all	b	b	y
Parkinsonia aculeta (Jerusalem Thorn)	e	1,3,5,6,7	b	b	y
Peltaphorum inerme (Rusty Shieldbearer)	d	1,3,5,7	a	a	y
Phoenix dactylifera (Date Palm)	e	all	c	b	n
Prosopis juliflora (Mesquite)	e	all	b	b	n
Schinus terebinthifolia (Brazilian Pepper)	e	1,3,5,7	c	c	n
Tamarix aphylla (Athel Tree)	e	all	c	b	n
Terminalia catappa (Indian Almond)	d	1,3,5,7	c	c	n
Washingtonia robusta (Mexican Fan Palm)	e	1,3,5,6,7	c	a	n
Zizyphus jujuba (Jujube)	e	all	b	b	n

(Below left) *Azederacha indica* (Neem Tree), (below centre) *Terminalia catappa* (Indian Almond), (below right) *Zizyphus jujuba* (Jujube)

TREES FOR POOL AREAS AND PATIOS

THE SINGLE most desirable characteristic for trees in patio or pool areas is that they are 'clean'; that is, do not produce litter that will fall into a swimming pool or stain the patio surface. This litter, of course, consists of leaves, fruits, berries, flowers, and seeds. There is no such thing as a totally clean tree, but there are those that produce shade and yet very little litter. The following short list contains those trees in this category which are most desirable near a pool (there are not many of them in this part of the world). To determine the growth habits and climate zones, check the plant encyclopedia (see pp. 77-137).

> *Citrus* (providing the fruit is picked. Also bees can be a problem while the tree is in flower)
> *Cocos nucifera* (Coconut Palm)
> *Eucalyptus rudis* (Desert Gum; blue foliage)
> *Ficus benjamina* (Weeping Chinese Banyan)
> *Ficus nitida* (Indian Laurel)
> *Ficus religiosa* (Peepul Tree)
> *Jacaranda acutifolia* (semi-deciduous, allows the sun in the winter)
> *Morus alba* (Fruitless Mulberry, deciduous)
> *Phoenix dactylifera* (Date Palm)

In gardener's jargon there is a tree shape called a 'patio tree'. This is a small tree, pruned to a globe shape, with a single trunk, and branches starting about one metre (3ft) from the ground. Citrus and Ceratonia are well-suited to this shape.

For patio trees, we may expand our list a bit because often these can be planted with ground cover underneath them so that litter may not be so much of a problem. In addition to the above, we can add some of the more attractive flowering and deciduous varieties:

> *Bauhinia variegata* (Purple Orchid Tree. Flowering, deciduous)
> *Ceratonia siliqua* (Carob. Use male tree only)
> *Erythrina caffra* (Kaffirboom Coral Tree. Flowering, deciduous)
> *Koelruteria bipinnata* (Chinese Flame Tree. Flowering, deciduous)
> *Plumeria* (Frangipani. Flowering, semi-deciduous)

A word of caution: many flowering trees may be undesirable in these situations, because they attract bees. There are also many attractive trees which have been excluded because they have thorny branches.

opposite page: main illustration *Phoenix dactylifera* (Date Palm), (top left) *Parkinsonia aculeta* (Jerusalem Thorn), (top right) *Pithecolobium dulce* (Manila Tamarind), (bottom right) *Schinus molle* (California Pepper), (bottom left) *Azederacha indica* (Neem Tree). This page: (left) *Ficus nitida*, (centre) *Ficus benjamina* (Weeping Chinese Banyan), (right) *Citrus*

(top) *Bauhinia
variegata* (Purple
Orchid Tree),
(right) *Cocos nucifera*
(Coconut Palm),
(above) *Eucalyptus
rudis* (Desert Gum)

HEDGES, SCREENS AND WINDBREAKS

PLANTS for these purposes can be divided into 3 groups: small shrubs or large ground covers up to 1m (3ft), clipped or natural, that can be used as borders for walkways or flower beds; medium-sized shrubs, from 1-3m (3-10ft), to border driveways or roadways, separate sections of property, or to screen a wall. These also can be left natural or can be clipped to achieve a more formal look. The third group consists of large plants suitable for wind breaks; these may be big shrubs, but more generally are trees, 3m (10ft) high or larger. Most fulfil these functions naturally, with little or no pruning.

Casuarina equistifolia (Beefwood)

plant	climatic zones	small	medium	large	clipped	natural
Acacia decurrens (Green Wattle)	1,3,5,7			*		*
Acacia farnesiana (Sweet Acacia)	all			*		*
Atriplex, various	1,3,5,7	*	*			*
Callistemon citrinus (Lemon Bottlebrush)	all but 6		*		*	*
Carissa grandiflora (Natal Plum)	1,3,5,7		*		*	*
Casuarina equistifolia (Beefwood)	all			*		*
Cistus (Rockrose)	all but 6		*			*
Clerodendron inerme (Wild Jasmine)	all		*		*	*
Cytisus praecox (Moonlight Broom)	all but 6		*			*
Dodonea viscosa (Hopseed Bush)	all		*		*	*
Eucalyptus, various	all			*		*
Euonymous japonica (Evergreen Euonymous)	all		*		*	*
Feijoa sellowiana (Pineapple Guava)	1,3,5,7		*	*	*	*
Hibiscus rosa-sinensis (Chinese Hibiscus)	1,3,5,7		*			*
Kochia scoparia (Summer Cypress)	all	*	*		*	*
Lantana camara	all		*		*	*
Lavandula (Lavender)	all	*	*		*	*
Leucophyllum frutescens (Texas Sage)	all		*			*
Malvaviscus arboreus	1,3,5,7		*			*
Nerium oleander (Oleander)	all		*		*	*
Pelargonium, various (Geranium)	all but 6	*	*			*
Photinia	all		*			*
Pinus halepensis (Aleppo Pine)	2,4,7			*		*
Plumbago capensis (Cape Plumbago)	all but 6		*			*
Podocarpus macrophylla (Yew Pine)	all but 6		*	*	*	*
Poinciana (Caesalpinia)	1,3,5		*			*
Prosopis (Mesquite)	all			*		*
Punica granatum (Pomegranate)	all		*		*	*
Santolina chamaecyparissus (Lavender Cotton)	all	*			*	*
Schinus molle (California Pepper)	all			*		*
Tamarix (Tamarisk)	all			*		*
Tecoma stans (Yellow Trumpet Flower)	1,3,5,7		*			*
Tecomaria capensis (Cape Honeysuckle)	1,3,5,7		*			*
Teucrium chamaedrys (Germander)	all	*	*		*	*
Thevetia peruviana (Yellow Oleander)	1,3,5,7		*		*	*
Xylosma congestum	all but 6		*		*	*

SHRUBS

(top) *Poinciana pulcherima* (Barbados Pine), (above) *Punica granatum* (Pomegranate), (above right) *Oleander*

SHRUBS EXIST in a wide range of shapes, sizes, leaf textures, flower colours and growth habits. For the Middle Eastern gardener there is happily a large variety to choose from in order to achieve the desired effect. Some can be clipped into dense formal hedges, others are airy and open-branched. Shrubs can be grown with flowers that encompass every colour in the spectrum. The height and spread available range from 50cm to 6m (2-20ft) or larger. Some, like white oleander and the poinciana, can be pruned to a single-trunk tree shape. The smaller varieties can serve as a ground cover.

Some of the more popular varieties are listed below with a brief description of each. For further details, see the plant encyclopedia (pp. 77-137).

plant	climatic zones	description
Arundo donax (Giant Reed)	1,3,5,7	Bamboo-like vertical clumps to 5m (15ft)
Atriplex, various	all	Excellent desert plants: drought- and salt-tolerant
Callistemon citrinus (Lemon Bottlebrush)	all but 6	Bright red, brush-type flowers. Grows to 3m (10ft)
Canna	all	Long, wide, leathery leaves, many different colours available
Carissa grandiflora (Natal Plum)	1,3,5,7	White starlike flowers, small reddish fruit
Cassia, various	1,3,5,7	Small-leafed, yellow blossoms
Chrysanthemum frutescens (Marguerite Daisy)	all	White, yellow, pink flowers (Florist's Mum)
Chrysanthemum morifolium ('Florist's Mum')	all but 6	Florists' chrysanthemums
Cistus, various (Rockrose)	all	Showy white, yellow, purple flowers
Cortaderia selloana (Pampas Grass)	all	Large distinctive grass clumps with feathery plumes
Cytisus, various	all	Compact, small-leafed, yellow flowers

plant	climatic zones	description
Dahlia, various	all	Bright, multicoloured annual flowers; 30cm to 1m (1-3ft) high
Echium fastuosum (Pride of Madeira)	all	Lavender blue flower spikes, fleshy leaves
Eleagnus pungens (Silverberry)	all	Large, rangy, silver-green foliage
Feijoa sellowiana (Pineapple Guava)	1,3,5,7	To 2.5m (8ft). Red and white flowers, tasty fruit
Helianthus annuus (Sunflower)	all	Huge yellow and brown flowers
Hemerocallis (Day Lily)	all	Yellow, orange, red lilies
Hibiscus rosa-sinensis (Chinese Hibiscus)	1,3,5,7	Reliable large shrub; showy variety of colours
Kochia scoparia (Summer Cypress)	all	Feathery, fern-like columns to 1.5m (5ft)
Lantana camara	all but 6	Versatile medium-sized shrub; many colours available
Leucophyllum frutescens (Texas Sage)	all	Medium-sized shrub, grey foliage
Limonium perezii (Statice)	1,3,5,7	Small shrub; beautiful lavender-blue flowers
Malvaviscus arboreus	1,3,5,7	Forefather of hibiscus; tubular red flowers
Moraea (Fortnight Lily)	1ll	Upright, long narrow leaves; orchid-like blooms
Nandina domestica (Heavenly Bamboo)	all	Bamboo-like shade plant; varicoloured foliage
Nerium oleander (Oleander)	all	Old, reliable flowering shrub
Pelargonium (Geranium)	all	Wide variety of flower colours
Phormium tenax (New Zealand Flax)	1,3,5,7	Bold, sword-like tall leaves
Photinia	all	To 3m (10ft); glossy dark-green leaves
Plumbago capensis (Cape Plumbago)	1,3,5,7	Large, round shrub: light blue flowers
Poinciana (Caesalpinia)	1,3,5	Fine-leafed, red, yellow flowers
Punica granatum (Pomegranate)	all	Popular, small-leafed, hardy shrub
Ricinus communis (Castor Bean)	all	Attractive foliage, but highly poisonous
Tecoma stans (Yellow Trumpet Flower)	1,3,5,7	Large shrub; showy, yellow trumpet blooms
Tecomaria capensis (Cape Honeysuckle)	1,3,5,7	Small-leafed, orange tubular flowers
Thevetia peruviana (Yellow Oleander)	1,3,5,7	Thin, narrow leaves; yellow-cream flowers
Xylosma congestum	all but 6	Bronze foliage turning to green; versatile shrub

(from left to right):
Dodonea viscosa
(Hopseed Bush);
Malvaviscus arboreus;
Carissa grandiflora
(Natal Plum);
Hibiscus rosa-sinensis
(Chinese Hibiscus)
(centre), flanked by
Catharanthus rosea
(Madagascar
Periwinckle)

GROUND COVERS

Gazania splendens

GROUND COVERS can perform a variety of functions in a landscape. They can act as a lawn substitute, giving an attractive, even, green effect, without requiring frequent mowing. Perennials and annual bedding plants can provide year-round colour. Mixing shapes and sizes can produce a natural effect almost like the floor of a European forest. Finally, the more drought-tolerant species can be used for sand stablization where the desert encroaches on a city or village.

Most of the plants in the table below are perennials. A few horizontal-growing annual bedding plants are listed, but most annuals are shown in the section 'flowers by colour and by duration' (see pp. 39-42). Further details on each species are given in the plant encyclopedia (see pp. 77-137).

plant	climatic zones	description
Acacia ongerop	all	Excellent desert ground cover. Hardy, very drought- and salt-tolerant. Spreads to 5m (15ft)
Ajuga reptans (Carpet Bugle)	all	Some varieties have most unusual bronze foliage
Alternanthera versicolor	1,3,5,7	New foliage is a distinct red colour
Anthemis nobilis (Chamomile)	all	Annual. A green, smooth carpet
Arctotheca calendula (Cape Weed)	1,3,5,7	Grey-green foliage, yellow daisy-like flowers
Asparagus sprengeri (Asparagus Fern)	all	Hardy, feathery, wide-spreading clumps
Atriplex, various	1,3,5,7	Ground covers and small shrubs, some with blueish-grey foliage. Highly drought-, salt-tolerant
Bougainvillaea spectabilis	all	Some varieties are wide-spreading, 40-60cm (16-24in) high
Carissa grandiflora 'Green Carpet' (Natal Plum)	1,3,5,7	Deep green, small-leafed low spreader; star-like white flowers
Catharanthus rosea (Vinca rosea) (Madagascar Periwinkle)	all	Small, spreading shrub; red and white flowers
Convolvulus (Ground Morning Glory)	all	Leggy, informal, blue flowers
Festuca ovina glauca (Blue Fescue)	all	Blue-grey grassy clumps
Gazania, various	all but 6	Showy, multi-coloured flowers almost year-round
Hedera canariensis (Algerian Ivy)	all	Hardy, large-leafed ivy
Iberis sempervirens (Candytuft)	all but 6	Annual, profuse white flowers
Ice Plant		
Carpobratus edulis (Hottentot Fig)	all	A heavy succulent; pink and white scattered flowers
Delaspermum alba (White Ice Plant)	1,3,5,6,7	Good lawn substitute. Scattered small white flowers
Drosanthemum hispidum (Rosea Ice Plant)	1,3,5,7	Good for banks
Lampranthus spectabilis	1,3,5,7	Spectacular pink, orange, red, purple flowers
Malephora crocea	1,3,5,6,7	Nice even cover. Reddish-orange flowers
Ipomoea biloba (Goat's Foot Creeper)	all	Fast-spreading, vining trumpet flowers
Lantana montividensis (Trailing Lantana)	all	Bright lavender flowers almost all year round
Pelargonium peltatum (Ivy Geranium)	all but 6	Ivy-like leaves, wide variety of flower colours
Petunia hybrida	all	Annual with wide range of colours
Portulaca grandiflora (Rose Moss)	all	Succulent, many different colours
Verbena peruviana	1,3,5,7	Small-leafed, red flowers

(left) *Catharanthus rosea* (Madagascar Periwinkle), (far left) *Drosanthemum hispidum* (Rosea Ice Plant) and *Lampranthus spectabilis*

Malephora crocea

VINES AND OTHER CLIMBERS

VINES AND CLIMBERS are particularly important in Middle Eastern gardens because they are usually the most effective way to cover or soften the walls surrounding each villa or compound. But they need not be confined to walls. They can be most dramatic when climbing up and over an arbor or trellised pavilion. Some serve very well as a flowering ground cover. Fruit-producing vines, such as grapes and some melons, can be carefully trained onto an open framework to provide both decoration and food.

A combination of plants, flowers and man-made structures can provide some of the most pleasing and dramatic effects found in any garden.

(top) Ipomoea biloba (Goat's Foot Creeper), (above) Clerodendron inerme (Wild Jasmine)

plant	climatic zones	description
Antigonon leptotus (Coral Vine)	all	Semi-deciduous. Will climb 10m (33ft). Deep green foliage, pink flowers
Bougainvillaea spectabilis	all	Hardy. Wide range of profuse, brilliant blooms
Clematis armandii (Evergreen Clematis)	1,3,5	Sensitive to salts. Needs frequent pruning. Glossy leaves, white, fragrant flowers
Clerodendron inerme (Wild Jasmine)	all	Lush foliage; small white flowers
Clytostama callistegioides (Lavender Trumpet Vine)	1,3,5,7	Marginal in the hottest areas; does well in shade. 8cm (3in) lavender flowers
Doxantha unguis-cati (Cat's Claw Vine)	all	Very fast grower, easily supported; yellow, trumpet-like flowers
Gelsemium sempervirens (Carolina Jasmine)	all	Small-leafed, yellow flowers
Grape, various	all	Deciduous; good for arbors: varieties are listed in plant encyclopedia
Ipomoea biloba (Goat's Foot Creeper)	all	Very fast grower; needs support. Pink, lavender flowers
Jasminum (Jasmine)	all	Difficult to get started: fragrant white blooms
Lonicera japonica 'Haliana' (Hall's Honeysuckle)	all	Cut back hard once a year; fragrant white flowers
Passiflora (Passion Flower)	1,3,5,7	Striking, multi-coloured flowers; needs pruning to keep it neat
Quisqualis indica (Red Jasmine)	1,3,5,7	Bright red, jasmine-like flowers; fragrant

How to train vines and climbers

Where you have open trellises or arbors, training vines upward or laterally is relatively easy. As each stem gets longer, bend it carefully and push it through one opening, then back through another, higher opening, like a weave. An open-weave trellis can either be made or purchased. It is advisable to use one that is a similar height to your wall.

If you are training a vine against a blank wall, two rows of concrete nails can be nailed up the wall at 50cm (20in) intervals, with a wire strung between them: the vine is then tied to the wire. Take care when tying the vine: the best thing to use is a stretchable green vinyl tape. If this is not available, then tie the vine loosely with a string, so that the string will not choke the stem as it increases in girth.

There is another method of 'pulling' vines up a wall that is popular in the

(above)
*Bougainvillaea
spectabilis*, (right)
*Clytostoma
callistegioides*
(Lavender
Trumpet Vine),
(far right) *Lantana
camara*

Middle East. Tie one end of a 2-metre (6ft) piece of string to the vine and tie a rock to the other end. Throw the rock over the wall, and it will pull the stem upward. You should, however, carefully check outside the wall first, to ensure no passing pedestrian becomes the unwitting recipient of your rock.

CONTAINER PLANTS

Plants in pots add colour and interest to gardens of all sizes

THE VERSATILITY and ease of movement of container plants make them useful in a garden or patio. If you want to add a spot of annual colour to a corner, you can easily do it with flowering plants in a decorative ceramic pot, or cover a stretch of bare wall by putting a small tree or shrub in a wooden tub or box. A cluster of herbs in various-sized clay pots will also add interest to a drab area. If your apartment or villa has very little bare ground for planting, an assortment of containers filled with shrubs and flowering plants will liven it up. Some plants, like gardenias, will not tolerate the summer heat, and should be moved indoors near a window during the hotter months. Others like the winter sun and summer shade. A movable container is the best answer.

The tables below are broken down into three categories of container sizes – small, medium, and large, with brief descriptions of the plants recommended for each size.

Small containers 20cm (8in) diameter or smaller			
Annual flowers			Annuals do well in pots. Listed below are some of those best adapted to the climate
Calendula officinalis (Pot Marigold)	all	sun	Yellow and orange flowers
Celosia (Cockscomb)	all	sun	Annual; bright red plumes
Gazania, various	all	sun	Multi-coloured flowers
Petunia hybrida	all	sun	Annual; rich variety of colours
Salvia splendens (Scarlet Sage)	all	sun	Annual; lavender, pink, red blossoms
Tagetes (Marigold), various	all	sun	Annual; bright yellow, orange flowers

Medium containers 20-40cm (8-16in) diameter

plant	climatic zones	sun or shade	description
Aloe, various	1,3,5,7	both	Interesting, vertical, fleshy succulents
Asparagus sprengeri (Asparagus Fern)	1,3,5,7	both	Cascading, fern-like foliage
Canna	all	sun	Tall leathery leaves, multi-coloured blooms
Cassia nodosa	1,3,5,7	sun	Dense shrub, yellow flowers
Cestrum nocturnum (Night-blooming Jasmine)	1,3,5,7	both	Powerful night-time fragrance; needs summer shade
Chrysanthemum, various	all	sun	Most varieties need staking; wide variety of flower colours
Cistus purpureus (Orchid Rockrose)	all	sun	Compact, slow grower; reddish, purple flowers
Cytisus (Genista) racemosa (Scottish Broom)	1,3,5,7	sun	Dense shrub: yellow flowers
Gardenia, various	1,3,5,7	shade	Will take some winter sun. Move indoors in summer
Hemerocallis (Day Lily)	all	sun	Vertical, narrow leaves; yellow, orange blooms
Kochia scoparia (Summer Cypress)	all	both	Annual. Dense, feathery foliage. Columnar
Lantana montividensis (Trailing Lantana)	all	sun	Cascades over container; lavender flowers all year round
Pelargonium (Geranium)	1,3,5,7	sun	Wide variety of colours; prune often to keep compact
Rosa (Rose)	all	sun	Many flower colours. Deciduous; needs frequent pruning
Sanseveria trifasciata (Mother-in-Law's Tongue)	all	both	Tall, narrow, variegated leaves. Avoid frost if in zones 2,4
Senecio cineraria (Dusty Miller)	all	sun	Grey foliage, yellow flowers

Large containers 40cm (16in) diameter and bigger

plant	climatic zones	sun or shade	description
Citrus, various	all but 6	sun	Dwarf varieties are excellent for large pots, boxes
Ficus benjamina (Weeping Chinese Banyan)	1,3,5	both	Likes sun in winter, shade in sumer
Fruit trees, deciduous	2,4,7	sun	Dwarf varieties, particularly peach and nectarine
Hibiscus	1,3,5,7	sun	Striking flowers. Will need transplanting after four or five years
Nandina domestica (Heavenly Bamboo)	all	both	Winter sun, summer shade. Red and green foliage
Nerium Oleander (Oleander)	all	sun	Keep pruned to desired shape and size
Phormium tenax (New Zealand Flax)	1,3,5,7	sun	Tall, sword-like, bronzy leaves
Plumeria (Frangipani)	1,5	sun	Needs a large pot or box. This is the fragrant Hawaiian *lei* flower
Podocarpus macrophylla (Yew Pine)	1,3,5,7	sun	Small, narrow leaves. Dense, deep green
Punica granatum (Pomegranate)	all	sun	Dwarf varieties will give you pomegranates from a potted plant
Thevetia nerifolia (Yellow Oleander)	1,3,5,7	sun	Delicate foliage. Creamy yellow flowers
Vitex agnus-castus (Chaste Tree)	all	sun	Semi-deciduous. Spikey, lavender blooms
Yucca, various	1,3,5,6,7	both	Rigid, fleshy, sword-like leaves

FLOWERS BY COLOUR AND DURATION

Calendula officinalis
(Pot Marigold)

THE ABUNDANCE of colourful and exotically scented flowering plants which can be grown in the Middle East makes it possible to create outstanding gardens. To do this, however, takes careful planning. To enjoy summer colour, planting must take place in the autumn or spring, and the overall garden scheme must be conceived before that. It is possible to have some plants in flower every month of the year, but it takes a well-organized plan of sowing seeds, planting seedlings, and removing fading plants to do it.

Generally speaking, flowering plants should be planted in the autumn or early spring, and bulbs only planted in the autumn. In zones 1, 3, and 5, however, planting can be done at any time, but try to avoid midsummer.

Note: The following tables provide a guide to the approximate length of the flowering season for a wide selection of popular plants. For those readers who are new to the Middle East, an explanation is due regarding the traditional signs of the seasons you are accustomed to recognizing in plants. A mild winter climate, and extended summer heat, can produce erratic results in flowering schedules. In areas with well-defined seasons, such as Europe, plants will act as a seasonal time keeper. The bright yellow of forsythia in late February to mid-March tells you spring is just around the corner, the wide colour spectrum of primrose means warm weather has finally arrived, and the spectacular autumn colours of maples and dogwoods indicate winter is near. If you are used to these tell-tale signs of the seasons, the climate, and plants' reaction to it in this part of the world, will fool you.

For example, the willow acacias (*A. saligna*), which would normally show their yellow blossoms in California in March, may bloom along the Gulf in mid-December, following a November cold spell, then bloom again in April. The red-flowering *Malephora* ice plant may bloom at random times throughout the year, some years showing its most profuse colour in mid-winter. Bougainvillaea may be at its brightest in late autumn or early winter, rather than spring. Traditional spring-summer annuals, such as marigolds and petunias, can be grown all year.

For this reason flowering seasons have not been listed for many entries in the plant encyclopedia. In this part of the world, you really can have one long, year-round flowering season in your garden.

Duration of bloom is defined as follows: *short* is two weeks to two months; *medium* is two to four months; *long* is four months and longer. Check the plant encyclopedia for further details of each species.

	climatic zones	duration of bloom	blue	lavender	orange	pink	red	violet	white	yellow	multi
ANNUALS											
Antirrhinum majus (Snapdragon)	all	long	*		*	*	*	*	*	*	
Calendula officinalis (Pot Marigold)	all	long			*					*	
Celosia (Cockscomb)	all	med			*	*	*	*		*	*
Dianthus, various	all	long				*	*	*	*		*
Gomphrena globosa (Globe Amaranth)	all	med						*			
Helianthus annuus (Sunflower)	all	long			*					*	
Helichrysum bracteatum (Strawflower)	all	med			*	*	*		*	*	*
Iberis sempervirens (Candytuft)	all but 6	long							*		
Lobularia maritima (Sweet Alyssum)	all	long	*	*	*			*	*		
Papaver nudicale (Iceland Poppy)	all	short			*	*	*		*		
Petunia hybrida	all	long	*	*		*	*	*	*		*
Portulaca grandiflora (Rose Moss)	all	long			*	*	*	*	*		*
Salvia splendens (Scarlet Sage)	all	long			*		*	*			
Tagetes (Marigold), various	all	long			*					*	
Tropaeolum majus (Nasturtium)	all	med			*	*	*		*	*	*
PERENNIALS											
Agapanthus africanus (Lily of the Nile)	1,5,7	med	*						*		
Canna	all	long				*	*	*	*		
Carpobratus edulis (Hottentot Fig)	all	med			*					*	
Catharanthus rosea (Vinca rosea) (Madagascar Periwinkle)	all	long				*	*		*		
Chrysanthemum morifolium (Florists' Mum)	all but 6	med			*	*	*	*	*	*	*
Drosanthemum hispidum (Rosea Ice Plant)	1,3,5,7	med			*						
Gazania, various	all but 6	long				*	*	*	*	*	*
Lampranthus (Ice Plant)	1,3,5,7	long				*	*	*	*		
Lantana montividensis (Trailing Lantana)	all	long			*						
Limonium perezii (Statice)	1,3,5,7	long			*			*		*	*
Osteospermum fruiticosum (Trailing African Daisy)	all but 6	long			*			*	*		

	climatic zones	duration of bloom	blue	lavender	orange	pink	red	violet	white	yellow	multi
SHRUBS											
Callistemon citrinus (Lemon Bottlebrush)	all but 6	long					*				
Cassia	1,3,5,7	med								*	
Chrysanthemum frutescens (Marguerite Daisy)	all	long				*			*	*	
Datura (Angel's Trumpet)	1,3,5,7	long				*			*	*	
Echium fastuosum (Pride of Madiera)	all	long	*					*			
Feijoa sellowiana (Pineapple Guava)	1,3,5,7	med				*					
Gamolepsis chrysanthemoides	all	long								*	
Hibiscus rosa-sinensis (Chinese Hibiscus)	1,3,5,7	long			*	*	*		*	*	*
Jasminum mesneyi (Primrose Jasmine)	all but 6	med								*	
Jasminum sambac (Arabian Jasmine)	1,3,5	long							*		
Lantana camara	all	long			*	*	*		*	*	*
Nerium oleander	all	long				*	*		*		
Plumbago capensis (Cape Plumbago)	all but 6	med	*								
Poinciana (Caesalpinia)	1,3,5,	med				*				*	
Rosa (Rose)	all	long			*	*	*	*	*	*	*
Tecoma stans (Yellow Trumpet Flower)	1,3,5,7	long								*	
Tecomaria capensis (Cape Honeysuckle)	1,3,5,7	long			*		*				
Thevetia peruviana (Yellow Oleander)	1,3,5,7	long			*					*	
TREES											
Acacia baileyana (Bailey Acacia)	1,3,5,7	short								*	
Albizzia julibrissin (Mimosa)	all	short				*					
Bauhinia, various	1,3,5,7	short			*	*	*	*			
Callistemon viminalis (Weeping Bottlebrush)	all but 6	med					*				
Cassia didymobotrya	1,5	med								*	
Citrus, various	all but 6	short							*		
Delonix regia (Royal Poinciana)	all but 6	short			*		*				
Erythrina (Coral Tree)	1,3,5,7	short			*		*				
Fruit Trees, Deciduous	2,4,7	short				*	*		*		
Jacaranda acutifolia	all but 6	short	*								
Koelruteria	all but 6	med			*				*		
Lagerstroemia indica (Crape Myrtle)	2,3,4	med			*	*	*		*		
Melaleuca	1,3,5,7	short				*				*	
Melia azederach (China Berry)	all	short			*				*		
Moringa oliefera (Drumstick Tree)	1,3,5,7	short							*	*	
Parkinsonia aculeta (Jerusalem Thorn)	1,3,5,6,7	short								*	
Plumeria (Frangipani)	1,5	med			*	*			*		
Robinia pseudocacia (Black Locust)	all but 6	short							*		
Thespesia populnea (Aden Apple)	1,5,7	short					*				
Vitex agnus-castus (Chaste Tree)	all	med	*	*							

	climatic zones	duration of bloom	blue	lavender	orange	pink	red	violet	white	yellow	multi
VINES											
Antigonon leptotus (Coral Vine)	all	med				*					
Bougainvillaea spectabilis	all	long		*	*	*	*		*		
Doxantha unguis-cati (Cat's Claw Vine)	all	short								*	
Gelsemium sempervirens (Carolina Jasmine)	all	med								*	
Ipomoea biloba (Goat's Foot Creeper)	all	long		*		*					
Jasminum (Jasmine)	all	long							*	*	
Lonicera japonica 'Haliana' (Hall's Honeysuckle)	all	med		*	*	*			*	*	
Passiflora (Passion Flower)	1,3,5,7	med		*		*			*		
Quisqualis indica (Red Jasmine)	1,3,5,7	med					*				

(right) *Tecoma stans* (Yellow Trumpet Flower), (far right) *Bougainvillaea spectabilis*

FRAGRANT PLANTS

WHILE SITTING on your garden patio at night, have you ever enjoyed the fragrance of *Cestrum nocturnum* (Night-blooming Jasmine) wafted your way by a gentle breeze? If not you are missing an added bonus gardens can offer. Fragrant plants that do well in the Middle East are listed below.

name of plant	climatic zones	type of plant	type of fragrance
Anthemis nobilis (Chamomile)	all	ground cover	Crushed leaves produce pungent scent
Carissa grandiflora (Natal Plum)	1,3,5,7	shrub, ground cover	Citrus-like
Cestrum nocturnum (Night-blooming Jasmine)	1,3,5,7	vine	Powerful sweet fragrance at night
Citrus, various	all but 6	tree	Sharp pleasant fragrance
Clematis armandii (Evergreen Clematis)	1,3,5	vine	Delicate, sweet
Datura candida (Angel's Trumpet)	1,3,5,7	shrub	Musky night sce
Gardenia jasminoides (Gardenia)	1,3,5,7	shrub	The sweet scent of perfumes
Gelsemium sempervirens (Carolina Jasmine)	all	vine	Soft jasmine fragrance
Jasminum polyanthum (Pink Jasmine)	1,3,5,7	vine	The strongest-scented jasmine
Lantana montividensis (Trailing Lantana)	all	ground cover	Pleasant minty scent
Lavandula spica (English Lavender)	all	shrub	Nostalgic and ladylike
Lonicera japonica 'Haliana' (Hall's Honeysuckle)	all	vine	Sweet and heady
Mentha (Mint)	all	shrublet	A wide variety
Plumeria (Frangipani)	1,5	tree	The scent of Hawaiian *leis*
Quisqualis indica (Red Jasmine)	1,3,5,7	vine	Delicate jasmine
Robinia pseudocacia (Black Locust)	all but 6	tree	Clean, sweet
Rosa (Rose)	all	bush	Varies with varieties
Thymus (Thyme)	all	ground cover	Well-known herbal scent

Carissa grandiflora (Natal Plum)

FRUITS AND BERRIES

Schinus terebinthifolia
(Brazilian Pepper)

COLOUR IN A GARDEN need not, of course, consist solely of flowers. There are a variety of trees, shrubs and vines whose fruits or berries can add a bright accent to the landscape, particularly in the autumn and winter.

plant	climatic zones	description
Carissa grandiflora (Natal Plum)	1,3,5,7	Shrub; small, reddish-orange, plum-like fruit
Citrus, various	all but 6	Tree; see plant encyclopedia for various fruits
Eriobotrya japonica (Loquat)	all	Tree; sweet, aromatic, orange fruit with large seeds
Feijoa sellowiana (Pineapple Guava)	1,3,5,7	Large shrub; grey-green pineapple-flavoured fruit
Fruit Trees, deciduous	2,4	See plant encyclopedia
Grape, various	all	Vine; see plant encyclopedia
Melia azederach (China Berry)	all	Tree; the small berry-like, yellow-white fruits are poisonous
Photinia serrulata (Chinese Photinia)	all	Shrub; bright red berries in the autumn
Punica granatum (Pomegranate)	all	Semi-deciduous; the most popular Middle Eastern fruiting shrub
Schinus molle (California Pepper)	all	Tree; tiny, pepper-like berries in late summer and autumn; can be messy
Schinus terebinthifolia (Brazilian Pepper)	1,3,5,7	Tree; clusters of bright red berries
Zizyphus jujuba (Jujube)	all	Semi-deciduous tree; shiny, brownish-red fruits in the autumn, resembling dates

SECTION THREE
HOW TO GROW PLANTS
IN
THE MIDDLE EAST

HOW PLANTS GROW

Hibiscus cuttings

WHEN LANDSCAPING AND GARDENING, it is most helpful to have a basic knowledge of how plants grow. Plants are composed of water, proteins and various types of tissue which both consume and store energy. They are able to reproduce themselves and manufacture their own food.

The plant life cycle begins with a seed (except for ferns, mosses, fungi and algae, which develop from spores). The size and weight of seeds vary enormously, from the tropical Coca de Mer (*Lodicea Seychellarum*) whose seed may measure up to 50cm (20in) long and weigh 19kg (42lb), to epiphytic orchids in which there are over 35 millions seeds per ounce. Inside its protective shell or coating, each seed contains an embryo plant and a supply of stored food (protein, starch, oils) to get it started and sustain it until it is able to manufacture its own food. These stored foods give nuts, peas, beans and grains their nutritional value.

To encourage the seeds to germinate, or sprout, certain favourable conditions must be created. The most important of these are moisture and warmth. Certain varieties of seeds have other requirements: some need 'scarifying', in which the protective shell is removed by soaking in hot water or acid, or by scraping it off. Some require very high or very low temperatures, whilst others need a period of dormancy for up to two years. When germination occurs, the coating splits, a primary root starts downward into the soil, and a sprout with the seed leaves breaks the surface of the soil. The majority of seeds are dicotyledons, with two seed leaves, but many plants such as grasses, grains, bamboo, lilies, and others are monocotyledons with one leaf. Conifers have many seed leaves. Most seed leaves of different plants are very similar in appearance with a round to oval shape and may differ significantly from the mature leaves of the plant.

Plant parts: Roots

After the single root from the seed starts down into the soil, tiny white rootlets branch out and these absorb the water and nutrients needed for plant life and carry these substances to the rest of the plant. The nutrients are carried in a water-soluble form; if there is no water in the soil around the roots, the plant dies. As the plant matures and branches out, these rootlets enlarge, form their own rootlets, and assume a different appearance and function. The older portions near the stem grow a protective covering, resembling a smooth bark, and are used to transport water and nutrients, and also to anchor the plant in the soil.

The tip of the root is the point at which it grows, forming elongating cells that push ever deeper and farther into the soil to seek out moisture. Behind the root tip is a group of cells that produce single-celled root hairs. These are the cells that actually absorb the water and nutrients. These root hairs will die almost immediately if exposed to sunlight or dry air. This is why, in transplanting, it is important to keep as much of the soil around the roots (root ball) as possible when moving it, and to move it swiftly. Then water the plant immediately after the transplant.

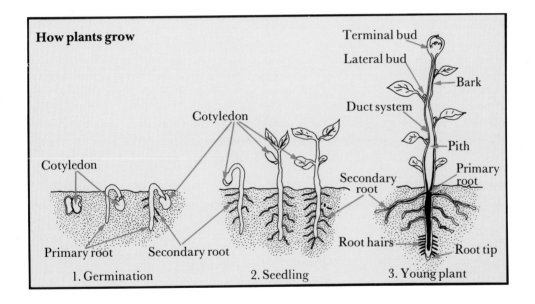

How plants grow

Terminal bud
Lateral bud
Bark
Duct system
Cotyledon
Pith
Cotyledon
Primary root
Secondary root
Cotyledon
Secondary root
Root hairs
Root tip
Primary root

1. Germination 2. Seedling 3. Young plant

Stems

As the seed leaves open up, they reveal the growth top, which then elongates and becomes the stem. Buds develop along the stem and then open up to produce the first true leaves. The stem continues to grow, and the upper end bud, called the terminal bud, carries the growth upward, while along the sides lateral buds form and develop into leaves or branches.

The main function of the stem is to transmit water and nutrients absorbed by the roots to the growing points (buds, leaves and flowers) and to return to the roots the food (sugars) manufactured in the leaves. This exchange is carried on by a complex duct system that extends from the root hairs to the growing points. In the stems of most plants this duct system is next to, and inside, the cambium layer, which is a group of cells just inside the plant's skin, or bark. This cambium layer

47

produces the cells that make up the duct system as well as the tissues that increase the girth of the plant. If wires, (such as those attached to plant labels) or string are wrapped around the stem and allowed to remain there as the girth increases, they can strangle the plant and eventually kill it.

Another important function of the stem is to provide rigidity or support. Many plants have quite rigid stems because the walls of their cells are stiffened by cellulose, lignin, and similar substances. In trees and large shrubs these stems become trunks, and the interior, dense heartwood serves solely as support, having outlived the function of conductive or storage tissue. In some plants, such as vines and some annuals, there is not enough woody tissue formed to support the plant, and they either need to be staked or trained onto trellises or walls.

Further functions of the stem are to store food during the dormancy period, to start growth in spring, and to aid in the development of seeds. Food, in the form of plant sugars, moves through the conductive system of the plant; when stored, it changes to starch, then in the spring when the plant is ready to resume growth, it is changed back to sugars for recirculation.

Many plants do not have a wood branch structure, but have instead underground modified stems such as bulbs, corms, tubers, or rhizomes. In these expanded stems sufficient food (starch) is stored to carry the plant through its dormant period and to start the new spring growth.

Leaves

The primary function of leaves is the manufacture of sugars and other carbohydrates throught the agency of chlorophyll. This converts carbon dioxide, water, and energy from the sun's rays into carbohydrates and oxygen. One of the great benefits of plants to human beings is that they produce and give off oxygen through their leaves. Without the oxygen, all animal life on earth would cease.

The conversion process, called photosynthesis, requires large quantities of water, which is drawn up through the stem from the roots and into the leaves. In the leaf tissue the water combines with carbon dioxide which has been drawn into the leaf from the air through minute breathing pores (stomata) on the underside of the leaf. In addition to allowing the inflow of carbon dioxide, the stomata also permit the outflow of water vapour and oxygen which are the by-products of the photosynthesis process.

During the dormant season of a plant, this process either slows considerably or stops altogether in the case of deciduous plants. During this cold weather period the requirement for water drops, and the roots no longer strain to keep up with the demands of the leaf system's manufacturing process. With the exception of palms, this is why it is wiser to transplant during the dormant period.

Flowers, fruit and seeds

Almost all plants produce flowers, but not all of these are easy to see. Some flowers are green and only on close scrutiny can be distinguished from the leaves. Others are hidden by the leaves or are so small they are almost undetectable. Within in the flower are the female parts (see diagram) called 'pistils', and when these are fertilized (pollinated) by the male cells (pollen) they produce seeds, often contained in fruit. The seeds then reproduce the plant.

The following descriptions of the various flower parts should help to clarify their respective functions.

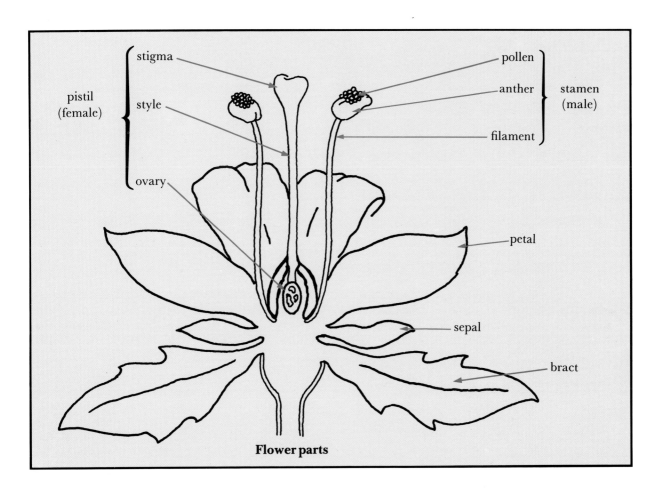

Flower parts

Bracts: Bracts are modified leaves that grow in a cluster around the flower. In some plants, like bougainvillaea, it is these bracts that produce the colour, and not the flower itself.

Sepals: These are the outer parts, usually green, that form a circle or cover around the newly formed flower bud, and peel downward to become generally insignificant when the flower opens. They are sometimes brightly coloured or hairlike, as in the bearded iris, and, when united before the bud opens, form a structure call the 'calyx'.

Petals: These generally are the largest and most colourful parts of the flower. Prior to the bud opening, they form a circle, called a 'corolla', underneath the sepals. Petals may be individual, as in hibiscus or roses, or tubular, as in petunias.

Segments: In certain plants, such as tulips and daffodils, the sepals and petals are all one structure, and this is called a 'segment'.

Stamens: The stamen is the male reproductive organ of a plant. Most stamens are composed of a stalk, called the 'filament', and on top of that, the 'anther'. The anther produces on its surface the fine dusty pollen, usually yellow, which is the male element used in the fertilization process. This pollen must be transferred to the female pistil to produce the fruit and seed of the plant. The transfer is usually carried out through the agency of the wind, or bees, or birds.

Pistils: These are the stalklike, female reproductive organs of the plant, and are typically positioned in the centre of the flower, with a swollen base called the

49

'ovary', which will eventually expand and become the fruit. At the top of the stalk, (or 'style') is the 'stigma' which typically receives the pollen.

Some plants contain both the male (stamen) and female (pistil) parts, and fertilization is accomplished when these parts are rubbed together by the wind. Others, for example most deciduous fruit trees, have only the male, or only the female parts. Here pollination must take place through the methods mentioned above. In extreme cases, such as the date palm, for pollination to be reliably successful, the pollen must be removed by hand from one tree, and carried over and placed on the pistil of another tree. There are men in the Middle East who are experts in this process.

SOILS AND PLANTING MIXES

The ideal soil is composed of dune sand, ground bark, complete fertilizer, and iron chelate

SOME MIDDLE EASTERN AREAS covered in this book have excellent planting soil. Most renowned, of course, is the Nile valley in Egypt and northern Sudan, where centuries of winter flooding have built up layers of rich alluvial silt. This process has been inhibited by the high dam at Aswan, but the area remains fertile. The Jordan River valley, with its banana plantations, also has excellent soil. Most of the soil throughout the Arabian peninsula, however, can only be described as bad for the purpose of supporting plant life. Exceptions include some of the mountainous areas, and areas below foothills where centuries of rain run-off have produced alluvial plains. The rest of the peninsula is primarily composed of limestone—calcium carbonate which causes high soil alkalinity. In some sensitive plants this will cause retarded growth, browning of the leaves, and, in extreme cases, death.

This problem makes life difficult for a gardener or landscaper, beacuse it is risky to use the indigenous soil. Through years of trial and error on various landscape projects, a highly successful type of soil mix has been developed. Basically it is 80-85% dune sand, and 15-20% organic material, preferably a ground or shredded tree bark. Dune sand is readily available in most areas, and has a number of advantages. Out in the desert it is windblown, and this tumbling action creates air spaces that are necessary in any good soil. This action also reduces the salt content, which is one reason the same sand is used in making concrete. The disadvantage is that such sand is very low in plant nutrients, thus requiring various fertilizers to be added. Alluvial soil from the wadis (dry stream beds) can be added to the sand, but this is somewhat risky because this clay and loam is often high in salt content.

A good planting soil has to have the ability to retain water and air, yet provide drainage. In a heavy clay soil, the minute particles are often so fine that there is very little or no drainage. The relatively large particles that constitute sand are just the opposite: water drains downwards too fast. Some material, then, needs to be added to the sand to hold some of the water around the roots of the plants, while letting excess water drain off. There are two basic types of material used – mineral and natural organic material.

Two of the mineral types, called Vermiculite and Perlite (actually insulating materials used in the walls of houses), are generally employed in nurseries as part of the soil used for propagating new plants from seed or cuttings, but are relatively expensive for a landscape soil mix. However, there is a product available called Agromusse, an organic resin foam, whose large, soft granules can be mixed into the soil. Agromusse is highly water absorbent. It also has the advantage of not breaking down chemically, as the natural organic products do. There is one type of Agromusse that has iron injected into it, but otherwise it is devoid of any nutrients. It is best used in combination with a natural organic material.

The three most commonly used natural organic materials are animal manure, peat moss, and ground or shredded bark.

Animal manure (sheep, chicken, or cow) is risky to use because unless it has been spread and dried in the sun, it may be too 'hot' (high in nitrogen-producing nitrates), and may therefore burn the plants. This can result in the leaves browning, retarded growth, and can even kill the plant. It may also contain unwanted weed seeds.

Peat moss is good to use, but decomposes faster, sometimes within six months, than the ground bark. It also needs to be broken up or run through a shredder to make it water retentive. Ground bark, most of which comes from Sweden or Germany, is the best to use. It does not decompose as quickly (lasting three to four years), is safe and mixes easily.

Because the sand and soil amendments are basically 'inert' (which means they lack plant nutrients), fertilizers should be added to the soil mix before planting (see pp. 64-5 for further details).

Soil mix table

The different soil mixes in the table below are listed in order of preference:

sand	other ingredients
80%	ground bark 20%
80%	ground bark 10%
	Agromusse 10%
80%	peat moss 10%
	Agromusse 10%
50%	ground bark 20%
	wadi soil 30%
85%	animal manure 15%
	(sun dried)

for containers	
60%	ground bark 20%
	Agromusse or Perlite 20%

Mixing the soil

The methods, tools and equipment needed to mix the soil will depend on the quantity. But whether it is one cubic metre or ten truckloads, first calculate the proportions and quantity of each ingredient, following the soil mix table (see p. 52) and the quantities in the fertilizer table (see p. 65).

For example, let us say you are mixing a small quantity: 1cu m/1.3yd (about 1350kgs/2970lb of sand). So using the two tables you would then need:

⅘cu m (1cu yd) sand
⅕cu m (1cu ft) ground bark
3 to 4 kg (6½-8½lb) Osmacote fertilizer
100gm (3oz) Sequestrene 138
500gm (15oz) Super Triple Phosphate

Spread the sand on the ground approximately 15cm (6in) thick, on top of that spread the ground bark 3cm (1in) thick, and then the three fertilizers evenly over the top. Moisten with water. Mix thoroughly with a square-point shovel.

For truckload quantities on a large landscape job, it is useful to know that most of the trucks delivering sand are of two sizes: the smaller, single-axle trucks carry 8cu m (10cu yd), the large, double-axle trucks carry 16cu m (20cu yd). If you are doing one large truckload your quantities would be:

16cu m (20cu yd) sand
3.2cu m (4cu yd) ground bark
50kg (110lb) Oxmacote fertilizer
1.6kg (3.5lb) Sequestrene 138
8kg (17.6lb) Super Triple Phosphate

Spread the sand on the ground approximately 50cm (20in) thick, on top of that spread the ground bark 10cm (4in) thick, and then the three fertilizers evenly over the top. Moisten, and mix thoroughly with a skip loader, lifting and dumping from all sides of the pile.

Heavy earthmoving equipment is needed for major landscaping projects

PLANTING

Planting a *Plumbago capensis* (Cape Plumbago)

IN THIS PART of the world, the most important aspect of planting is to have the right planting soil. Before you put any plants in the ground, ensure that the soil mix is suitable (see pp. 51-3).

The best time to plant is early autumn or early spring. However, it can be done successfully in midwinter in frost-free areas. Try not to plant in midsummer, but, if unavoidable, make sure you water immediately after planting, and frequently thereafter. You must expect a higher mortality rate from summer planting.

Plants from containers

Almost all of the plants that you buy in local nurseries will be in some kind of pot or container, most being in various-sized plastic pots. The most common approximate sizes are:

container size	plant size
Flats – 45×45×7cm (18×18×3in)	50-100 small ground cover or bedding plants
1 gallon pots (20cm/8in diameter)	single plants 30 to 50cm (12-20in)
5 gallon pots (30cm/12in diameter)	single plants 40 to 100cm (20-40in)
15 gallon pots (40cm/16in diameter)	trees up to 2m (6½ft)

For plants in the 1 gallon-size pots and larger, you will need to dig a hole at least twice as wide and twice as deep as the container, and haul away the dirt removed from the hole before backfilling with soil. Fill the hole with water, and let it drain. Next fill the bottom of the hole with your planting soil mix, and tamp it firmly in place so that the bottom of the root ball of the plant rests on the soil mix, and the top of the root ball is at ground level.

Now remove the plant from the plastic pot by turning the plant upside down while spreading your fingers across the top of the root ball. Firmly tap the bottom of the pot to loosen the root ball, then pull the pot upwards to disengage it from the root ball. This operation for a 5-gallon pot may take two people, and, because of its weight, a 15-gallon pot may require up to 4 people. Before pulling the pot off the root ball, make sure you prune off any roots growing through the drain holes in the bottom. It will make it easier to remove the pot if the root ball is moist, but not saturated. Some plants may come in strange varieties of metal cans. These cans will have to be cut all the way to the bottom on two sides with tin snips or shears and prised apart, before the root ball is lifted out. Be careful in this operation, as the cut edges are razor sharp, and can inflict a nasty cut. Where possible, avoid buying plants in metal cans, since they may have previously contained an injurious chemical. Also avoid plants that appear to be potted in heavy clay soil. These are less likely to suceed after planting.

Once the plant is out of the container, check to see if it is root bound. (If it is there will be large fleshy roots circling the soil ball and pressing into it.) If a plant is root bound, and the girdling roots are not loosened, future root growth can very easily be inhibited, and the top foliage portion of the plant may not grow much larger than its present size.

Place the plant onto the soil mix in the hole, being careful not to break, split, or crack the root ball. In some of the more sensitive desert plants, like eucalyptus, this can kill the plant by allowing an excess of air to the feeder roots. Then pour your planting mix inbetween the root ball and the sides of the hole, firmly tamping the soil in, and building a basin around the plant just outside the edge of the hole for watering. Fill the basin with water immediately, or at least within an hour or so, depending on the weather.

Seeds

Planting lawns from seed is explained in detail on pp. 58-9. To grow other types of plants from seed there are two basic procedures to follow:

If seeding directly into the ground, try to have at least 30cm (12in) depth of moistened planting soil mix in the seeding area. If you are seeding a herb or vegetable garden, or just want to create nice even rows, line out each row by stretching a string from one end of the area to the other. If possible, orient the rows in a north-south direction to allow for even sunlight. Alter the spacing of the rows according to the directions on the seed packets. Make a furrow underneath the string using the corner of a hoe, a knife, or just your finger, adjusting the depth as indicated on the seed packets. Open a corner of the seed packet and tap the seed slowly into the furrow, or empty the seed into your hand and pinch it evenly into the furrow. Cover the seed with the soil mix and tamp down evenly with your hand. Label each type of seed sown, using the seed packets on small stakes. If you are seeding 'free-form' drifts of flowers or ground cover, mix the seed with three or four times as much dry sand, then sow by hand evenly over the area. Cover with a 3-5mm ($\frac{1}{10}$-$\frac{1}{5}$in) layer of bark or peat moss as a mulch. Water as soon as possible after seeding is complete. You will then need to water lightly but frequently to keep the seed continually moist until it germinates and puts on its second set of leaves. This means watering 2 or 3 times per day in the cooler months, and 5 or 6 times per day in the summer months. If the seed is allowed to dry out just once, it will die. After sprouting, thin the plants out to the spacing recommended on the seed packets.

Because the watering requirements for seeds are different to those of adjoining planted areas, it may be best to start your plants in 'flats': 45×45×7cm (18×18× 3in) plastic or wooden trays. These may be available from a nursery, but if you

This newly rooted
Oleander cutting is
ready for planting

make your own flats, ensure they have narrow openings or small holes for drainage. Use a soil mix in the flats which is heavier in organic material than that used in a planting mix – about ⅔ sand, and ⅓ peat moss or ground bark. Sow the seed in even furrows, then cover with soil, and label each type of seed. Keep the soil moist, but not saturated, and expose it to ambient light, but not direct sunlight. After germination, plant the seedlings into the ground by carefully digging your finger into the soil around the roots of each seedling and pulling it out, starting at one corner of the flat. Place the seedling into a small hole in your planting soil, then firmly press the soil around the small root ball so that the top of the root ball is at ground level. Water thoroughly after planting.

LAWNS

FOR A LUSH, green, luxurious feeling in a landscape, there is nothing quite like a smooth, manicured carpet of grass. Lawns require larger quantities of water than other types of ground cover, and they need regular maintenance and attention by an experienced gardener. They are relatively rare in the Middle East, but they are possible.

Bermuda Grass and *Alternanthera versicolor*

Irrigation

To root properly and survive the heat, lawns need a well-designed irrigation system. Watering by hand, using a movable sprinkler connected to a hose, or just laying a hose on the ground and moving it about, produces spotty, uneven lawns. The irrigation system for a large grass area within a landscape project should be designed by a professional. But fortunately for the home gardener some nurseries and garden shops now stock do-it-yourself kits with sprinkler heads, underground tubing, and directions on installation, sprinkler spacing, and water pressure (see pp. 61-3). Like most plants, lawns should be watered deeply, and as infrequently as possible. Bear in mind, however, that they do need to be watered more often than other areas. Each watering with a proper irrigation system should last about twenty or thirty minutes, or until water run-off starts, to allow for deep water penetration. In zone 3 areas (see p. 12) during the summer months, an established lawn should be watered every other day, or at most once a day. In spring and autumn this can be reduced to once or twice a week. In the more humid coastal areas, at the higher elevations, and during the winter, a lesser watering frequency is required. Overwatering is to be avoided, as it enourages soil pests and root-destroying fungi.

Planting your lawn

The two most important aspects of making a lawn are watering (see above), and the preparation of the soil bed in which it is planted. Planting soils are described in a separate chapter (see pp. 51-3). While planning the grass area for your garden, you should allow for a depth of about 30cm (12in) of planting soil (topsoil). This may necessitate the removal of 30cm of the existing ground. For lawns, one of the best soil mixes is 80% dune sand, and 20% shredded tree bark. In addition to the fertilizers and micro-nutrients listed for planting soils, phosphate should be added to promote strong and rapid root growth.

Once your irrigation system is installed, you can commence spreading the top soil. For best results, first spread 7 or 8cm (3in) of soil over the area, then roto-till or dig this into the existing ground to avoid a 'soil interface' (two dissimilar soils meeting at a level plane). For large areas this roto-tilling can be done with a mechanical roto-tiller or a grader. A round point shovel is sufficient for smaller areas. Then spread the balance of the soil to a depth of 32cm (13in). The extra depth is to allow for compaction, either by a water-filled roller, if available, or just by the action of the water from the sprinklers. It is best to grade, or smooth out, the soil into a slight dome shape so that the centre of the lawn area is about 1% higher than the perimeter. In an area 10m (11yd) long, the centre, then, would be 10cm (4in) higher than the edge. This helps to prevent water collecting in shallow areas, and encourages run-off when necessary. The best way to smooth the soil is to use the back of a bow rake or level rake, the wider the better. Aluminium rakes up to 120cm (48in) wide are available for just this purpose. Break up or remove any clods of dirt during this process. If pop-up sprinkler heads are used, the soil level, after compaction, should be slightly higher than the top of the sprinkler to allow the lawn mower to pass over it safely.

After the top soil is installed and smoothed, it is time to do the planting. First test your irrigation system to make sure all the sprinklers are working and producing the right water pattern. This is also important because it moistens the soil, which will in any case be necessary before planting begins. Most lawns in the Middle East are common Bermuda grass (*Cynadon dactylon*), grown from seed. The seed can be scattered by hand or with a hand held 'whirlybird'-type mechanical spreader, at the rate of 3-4gm (0.1oz) per sq.m (1.2yd). It is best to spread the seed in the morning when winds are light, or on a windless day. Again, be sure the soil is moist before spreading. The best times of the year to start a lawn are early autumn and early spring. Success can also sometimes be achieved by sowing the seed in midsummer with careful watering, but avoid seeding in midwinter. After distributing the seed evenly, lightly rake it into the soil, then apply a thin layer (perhaps 5mm/⅕in), of shredded bark or peat moss over the seed as a mulch. Rake this lightly, working backwards to smooth out any footprints, or roll with a half-full roller.

Now comes the crucial part – watering for germination. Turn the sprinklers on immediately after seeding so you will soak the soil to a depth of 10-15cm (4-6in) (this should take about 10 or 15 minutes). From then on until the grass is about 5cm (2in) high, and ready to cut for the first time, you must keep the seed moist. If the seed dries out just once, it will kill it. This means watering during the cooler months 2 or 3 times a day, and in the hot summer months 5 or 6 times a day, with the first watering at 7.00 or 8.00 am, and the last about 8.00 or 9.00 pm. Each watering should last 10-15 minutes.

Some grasses, including the finer-leafed hybrid Bermudas, are planted as stolons (sprigs). The soil preparation and watering are the same for these as for seed. The stolons can be scattered over the soil at the rate of 1-6 bushels per 100 sq m (120yds), but the most successful way is to 'plug' them into the soil at about 15cm (6in) spacing. Then cover them with a thin layer of shredded bark or peat moss as a mulch.

Types of grass

Zoysia Grass

The types of lawns that will grow here are limited by the hot, windy climate, the alkaline soil, and the salty well water. The fine, cool-season grasses, such as bents and various fescues (found in Europe and the US), will only grow with a great deal of care in the higher elevations. It is therefore best to stick to those varieties that have proven themselves in the Middle Eastern environment. Each needs to be mowed every 1-2 weeks.

type of grass	method of planting	description
Common Bermuda	seed	Fine-leafed, spreads by runners to 2-3cm (1in). Builds up 'thatch' (a thick, brown, lower growth) which needs to be cut every 2-4 years.
Tif Green Bermuda	stolons	Fine-textured lawn, deep blue-green. Can be cut even lower than Common Bermuda. Used in golf greens.
Tif Dwarf Bermuda	stolons	Very dense and closely mowed. Spreads slower than Tif Green Bermuda.
Adelaide (Paspalum vaginatum)	seed	A good substitute for Bermuda. Very drought- and salt-tolerant.
Annual Rye	seed	Can be used to overseed Bermuda in winter if it goes dormant. Coarser: cut to 4-5cm (1½-2in). Dies out when Bermuda returns in the spring.
Zoysia	seed	A deep green, clumping grass, which requires only infrequent cutting. Do not plant in areas where it will be walked upon.

WATERING

PROBABLY the most difficult question to answer about gardening is 'how often should I water?'. The difficulty in answering lies in the large number of factors that affect a plant's water requirements: type of soil, size and depth of the root system, density of planting, and quality of the water are just a few of these. But the major factors in the Middle East that make proper watering so crucial are temperature, humidity, and wind. And of course the common conditions in the summer that dictate a need for lots of water, are extreme heat, low humidity and high winds. So, given these rather deleterious conditions, how often, and for how long, do we need to water?

The rule of thumb to use for watering any plants is: water deeply and infrequently. The purpose of long, deep watering is to produce a root system growing as far down, or as deeply, as possible. Thus, when the top 8-12cm (3-5in) of ground has dried out from evaporation and absorption, the deeper, cooler ground will still retain moisture to be absorbed by the root system. Also, in order to survive, plants need to absorb oxygen from the soil into the roots, so minute air spaces are required in the soil. If the ground is saturated from too frequent, shallow watering, there are no spaces between soil particles to allow for air. Also, if the soil remains low in oxygen, harmful micro-organisms can produce toxic substances, kill off beneficial bacteria, and produce fungus diseases. This is how plants die from overwatering. Deep watering, however, will help to leach the salts in the soil downward away from the root area.

To avoid this, and to make your watering problem easier, it is important to grow your plants in a soil as close as possible to one of those described on p. 52.

How often should you water?

Part of the answer lies in observing results in your own garden, and in sharing experiences with other gardeners. If the ground surface appears dry and cracked, and 10-12cm (4-5in) down the soil is still dry, it probably needs water. Drooping plants with dry, discoloured curling leaves are further evidence. On the other hand if the ground appears wet, and is saturated at 10-12cm (4-5in) you do not need to water. Overwatered plants may appear limp, and start dropping leaves.

The frequency table below is based on the climatic conditions in zone 3 (see p. 12). The watering frequency should be less in the more humid coastal areas and in the cooler areas of the peninsula. 'Shallow-rooted' plants include ground covers and small shrubs, 'medium-rooted' are large shrubs, small trees and vines. For deep-rooted large trees, the best watering method is to set a hose at the base of the tree, every month, and let water trickle into the ground for an hour or so. It also helps to have a soil basin around the tree reaching out to the drip line.

The figures refer to the number of days *between* waterings.

plant type	summer	spring/ autumn	winter
Lawns	1-2	3-7	7-10
Shallow-rooted plants	2-4	4-8	8-10
Medium-rooted plants	4-7	7-10	10-15

The difficulty, of course, is that most gardens contain a mixture of these plants and some sort of compromise must be reached.

How much water?

In a sandy soil mix (such as is recommended in this book) 2.5cm (1in) of water

(opposite page) The ancient method of irrigation is still used effectively today

will penetrate the soil approximately 30cm (12in). In a heavy clay soil, it takes about 6cm (2in) of rain to penetrate the same depth. The optimum penetration is about 60cm (24in) of penetration requiring about 5cm (2in) of water per week. But how can you tell when you have 5cm (2in) of water? Some sprinkler system manufacturers, such as Rainbird, whose products are sold in Saudi Arabia and the Gulf, have calculated precipitation rates, in inches per hour, for each of their sprinkler heads, and have this information in their catalogue. If you have a system installed for you, ask the contractor to provide this information at your particular water pressure. If you install your own, the dealer from whom you buy the equipment should provide it. Another relatively accurate way to determine precipitation is to put empty coffee cans or cups in the ground at varying distances from a sprinkler, and see how long it takes to fill each can to 2.5cm (1in). This will also tell you if you are achieving an even water distribution.

Most irrigation systems will take 30-90 minutes to deliver 5cm (2in) of water. However, leaving the sprinkler on for as long as this may well produce run-off and flooding in adjacent areas. So in order to get your 60cm (24in) of penetration per week, you may have to water as long as possible once, say for 40 minutes, followed by 1 or 2 other waterings of perhaps 15 minutes.

If a sprinkler system is not practical, and you have to irrigate the area with a hose, flood it as deeply as possible without having run-off. If you find that the water issuing from the hose is digging a channel in the soil, tie a folded piece of burlap or rubber to the hose end to help diffuse the heavy stream.

There is another easy rule of thumb to use in watering. If your plants look strong, green, and healthy, whatever you are doing is right, so keep it up.

FEEDING

The yellowing leaves on this *Catharanthus rosea* (Madagascar Periwinkle) indicate it is suffering from chlorosis (iron deficiency)

'FERTILIZER' is another name for the food, or nutrients, for a plant. It makes it grow, keeps it green, and helps to produce the flowers and fruit. The three basic fertilizer elements are Nitrogen (N), Phosphorus (P), and Potassium (K).

Nitrogen regulates a plant's ability to produce proteins which are needed to form new protoplasm in the cells. This is most evident in the young, tender plant tissues, such as new leaves, buds, and tips of shoots. Lack of Nitrogen is shown by the yellowing of the leaves, which eventually die and drop off.

Phosphorus, which is present in all living tissue, is required for photosynthesis and the transfer of energy within the plant. It is particularly useful in establishing a healthy root system in new plants.

Potassium is essential in the production and movement of starch and sugars, and also in the plant's cell-dividing growth cycle.

A 'complete fertilizer' (the most common variety) contains all three of these elements – the percentage of each should be designated on the bag or container. Thus a bag might show 10-10-6, meaning 10% available Nitrogen, 10% Phosphorus (P_2O^5) and 6% Potash (Postassium). Never use a chemical fertilizer unless these numbers are shown.

The other type of fertilizer your garden will need is micronutrients, particularly Iron (Fe). The other micronutrients are Zinc and Manganese. Only minute quantities of these are needed, but a deficiency of them causes a condition called 'chlorosis', in which the surface of the leaves turns yellow, whilst the veins remain green. Lack of Iron is the most common cause of chlorosis.

Most soils in the Middle East are very low in these nutrients, so a year-round fertilizing programme is necessary. The table below will help you to establish this programme. All products listed below are well-tried, and should be available.

fertilizer type	plant type	when to apply	amount	method	notes
Osmocote plus 16–18–5+ traces	general	every 9 months	1.5kg/10sq m (3.3lb/13sq yd)	Spread on soil, mix in to 10cm depth	Releases fertilizer over 9 month period. Best to apply in spring. Will last for entire season. Has micronutrients and is a complete fertilizer
Osmocote 16–17–5+ Fe	general	every 9 months	2kg/10sq m (4.4lb/13sq yd)	Same as above	Same as above but does not have micronutrients
Sierratabs 20–10–5+ traces	trees shrubs	every 2 years	1-2 tabs/shrubs 2-6 tabs/trees 400ml/100l. water	'Plant' tabs at 20cm depth around drip line of tree	Release over a 2 year period; will not burn plants. Also contains chelated micronutrients
Greenzit npk	all purpose	March–May Sept	400ml/100l. water (14fl oz/22.2 gal)	Liquid. Mix with water, spray in foliage	Gives quick greenery. This is a fertilizer for problem trees and shrubs
Greenzit npk	lawns	every month	200ml/100l. water (7fl oz/22.2 gal)	Spray on lawns 1 litre/10sq m	As above
Complete Fertilizer npk	all purpose			Follow directions on container	Do not overapply as it can burn easily
Urea 46–0–0	lawns date palms	when yellowing occurs	20-50gm/10sq m (0.7-1.5oz/12sq yd)	Spread on soil	Can cause severe burn. Use only if npk's (4-6 above) are not available
Triple Super Phosphate 0–46–0	all purpose	mix with soil	500gm/sq m (16oz/sq yd)	Mix well into planting soil	Very useful for turf. Very safe, and will not burn
Sequestrene 138 Fe (Iron Chelate)	all purpose	when chlorosis is observed	50gm/sq m (1.5oz/sq yd)	Spread on soil and water deeply, or apply as folial spray	Same micronutrients as in Osmocote plus. Use with general npk fertilizers
Soil sulphur	all purpose	mix with soil	1kg/1cu m (2.2lb/1.3cu yd)	Mix well into soil	Will lower pH of soil
Iron sulphur	all purpose	mix with soil	1kg/1cu m (2.2lb/1.3cu yd)	Mix well into soil	Will lower pH and add some iron

PEST AND DISEASE CONTROL

ONE OF THE MORE fortunate aspects of growing ornamental plants in the Middle East is that it is a relatively pest and disease-free environment. However, there are problem insects, fungi, and viruses, and you should know what they are, and how to control them. And as the vegetation throughout the Middle East increases, through both agriculture and horticulture, the pests will multiply too. This chapter will help you to identify them, and to keep your garden free of them.

Most pests and diseases will have to be eradicated with chemicals, but there are other measures that will help. Some insects and other animals help the gardener by preying on garden pests. Lizards, some beetles, lacewings, ladybirds and spiders all belong to this category.

It also helps to keep your garden neat and clean, since piles of dead leaves, clippings, and trash are breeding grounds for all kinds of insects and soil pests. But the most important defense is to grow a healthy, well-maintained garden. Plants are like people, the healthier they are, the more resistant to disease and organisms they are.

The more common pests and diseases found in this area are listed below, along with the best means of control.

PESTS	control	method of application
Aphids: tiny green, yellow, or pinkish-white insects found on leaves in colonies. Some excrete shiny honeydew. Can stunt plant growth.	Basudin or Malathion	Spray on leaves, particularly undersides. May need two applications.
Cutworms, armyworms: leaf- and grass-eating pests that feed at night and hide in the soil during the day.	hand picking; Basudin	Spray or drench soil where symptoms are visible in lawn bare spots or chewed leaves.
Earwigs: horn-tailed, night-feeding insects. Chew flowers and leaves. By day, live in soil, dark areas.	hand picking; bait with Baygon	Bait according to directions on container.
Mealy bugs: small, white cottony masses at stem joint or leaf bases.	Basudin or Pyrethrins	Spray where visible, check leaf undersides and roots.
Mites: colonies look like green, yellow, or red dust. Cause stippled leaves with silvery webs on underside.	Neoron or Kelthane	Spray leaves, especially underside.
Scale: colonies of small insects with black, brown or white protective shells. Mature shells have round dots. Secrete honeydew.	Supracide or Basudin or Malathion	Repeated spraying will be required. After third or fourth spraying, hose off with water spray.
Thrips: tiny flying insects that damage leaves, causing distortion. Feed on and distort flower buds.	Basudin or Malathion or Metasystox	Spray with Basudin, Malathion, or soil drench with Metasystox.

White Flies: small white insects which chew leaves. — Basudin or Malathion or Metasystox — Spray with Basudin, Malathion, or soil drench with Metasystox.

Date Palm Borer Beetles: bore holes in trunks and weaken base of petioles. — Supracide — Trunk spray or soil drench or injection. Should be done by professionals.

DISEASES	control	method of application
Phytophthora: soil-borne fungus that destroys roots, particularly those of date palms.	Ridomil	A wettable powder used to drench the soil. Follow directions on container.
Texas Root Rot: a fungus that thrives in alkaline soils. Destroys root parts causing wilting of leaves, particularly in lantana.	Ridomil or Soil Sulfur	Drench soil with Ridomil. Drill 10×60cm (4×24in) holes in affected soil, fill with 1 to 10 mixture of Soil Sulfur and ground bark or peat moss to lower soil Ph.
Powdery Mildew: white or grey fungus which appears on leaves, stems and flower buds as a powder or mealy substance. Prevalent in humid areas.	Tilt or Benomyl	Spray affected areas of plants.

Common garden pests

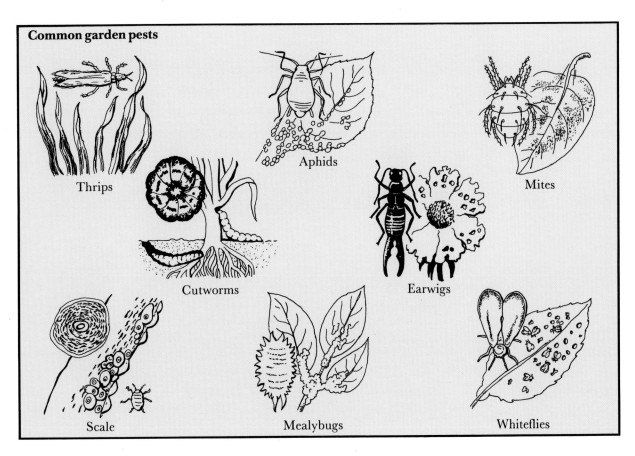

Thrips

Aphids

Mites

Cutworms

Earwigs

Scale

Mealybugs

Whiteflies

WEED CONTROL

When weeding,
ensure the entire
root system is
removed

BY DEFINITION, a weed is a plant that is growing where it is not wanted. A rose can be a weed, if it is not growing in its proper place. Most of the time, however, weeds are those uninvited garden guests which sprout up from seeds blown in by the wind or dropped by birds. The question is how to get rid of them.

The answer, unfortunately, is that the only practical way is by pulling them out by hand. The selective herbicides that kill grasses in ground cover areas, and kill broad-leaf weeds in lawns are not available in the Middle East at the time of writing. So your hand, trowel, or weeding hoe are the best means of getting rid of garden weeds. However, if you want to kill all the vegetation in a specific area, there are herbicides on the market here that will do the job.

Here are some tips on weeding that should make things a little easier for you:

1. Use the sandy soil mixes discussed on pp. 52-3. It is much easier to pull a weed, roots and all, out of a loose sandy soil than a heavy clay soil.

2. It is important that when you remove a weed, you take the entire root system with it. To help do this it is best to pull weeds, using just your hand, with a slow steady pulling pressure, 2-3 hours after you have watered. The added moisture in the soil helps the roots to slip out more readily. If the top of the plant breaks off when you pull it or cut it, the remaining root system may produce a new weed in a matter of days.

3. Try to do some weeding once or twice a week. This way, you will keep ahead of the weeds, pulling them out when they are still young and have not yet developed a tenacious root system.

4. If the stem of the weed breaks off, dig in the soil with a trowel, spade, or weeding hoe around the roots, then loosen and pull up.

5. Most weeds originate from seeds blown onto the soil or dropped by birds, so a solid covering over the ground will help keep the seeds from reaching the soil, and allow the heat of the sun to kill them off. One type of solid covering is ground cover plants, such as ice plant, african daisies, or trailing lantana, that will totally cover every square centimetre of ground. A 5cm (2in) covering of gravel mulch will do the same thing. Many landscape projects have both.

Lawns: Here are some preventive measures that will help keep weeds from appearing:

1. Cut your lawn regularly, once a week or every 10 days, and cut it long (3-5cm/1-2in), even Bermuda lawns. This will do a number of things: the longer, densely packed blades of grass will help keep the weed seeds from reaching the soil, and the longer grass will help shade the bare ground, resulting in a lower soil temperature. This will help keep damaging soil fungus from forming. Regular cutting keeps the grass denser, helping to crowd out weeds. If you have a Bermuda lawn that goes dormant in the winter, overseed it with annual Rye grass just when it starts to brown out. The annual Rye will spring up in a few days, so keeping your lawn fresh and green through winter, then die out in the spring as the Bermuda regrows.

2. A lush, healthy lawn will tend to keep weed seeds from germinating, and will crowd them out. So keep your lawn regularly fertilized through the growing season with Greenzit or a complete fertilizer. Each spring, and when you overseed with annual Rye grass in the winter, spread and water in Super Triple Phosphate to keep a deep healthy root system.

PRUNING

PRUNING CAN BE DEFINED as a method of directing plant growth by removing unwanted stems, leaves, and flowers. It is a widely misunderstood and neglected operation which can do a great deal to improve the neatness and appearance of your garden. In learning how to prune correctly, a little knowledge of how a plant grows can be helpful.

The terminal bud
At the end of each stem or branch there is a 'terminal bud', to which the plant's energy is directed to increase the length of that particular branch. If this terminal bud is removed (and it is easily done just by pinching it off with your thumbnail and finger), then growth will cease at that point, and the plant's energy will be directed to lower buds. The plant will then start producing new leaves or branches at these lower buds.

Thus, if you have a flowering plant, such as a zinnia, that is growing long and thin on one stem, pinch off the terminal bud just above the top set of leaves, and lower branches should form, making the plant wider and bushier.

Alternatively, you may have some branches on a shrub where most of the leaves are concentrated at the end of the branch. By pinching off the terminal bud, more leaves should appear in the lower, bare section of the branch.

Some trees, such as eucalyptus or poplars, tend to grow tall and thin, concentrating their energy on the main trunk or 'leader', as it is sometimes called. By cutting off the terminal bud of this leader, perhaps as far down as 50-60cm (20-24in) you will produce more side branches and make the tree bushier.

Where to prune
Here are the rules to follow:

1. Make your cut just above a branch junction, bud, or leaf node (where the leaf joins the stem). If you prune more than 1cm (1in) above the junction, the short length of stem left will die back to the joint, making it brown and unsightly, and may cause dieback even farther down the stem.

2. Cut just above a branch that faces towards an open space. Some shrubs when they are younger, such as *Tecoma stans* (Yellow Trumpet Flower), tend to grow outward, leaving an open space in the middle. In this case prune above a branch facing the interior of the plant. In all other cases thin out tangled branches in the interior so that new growth is upward or outward.

3. To produce a 'standard' single trunk tree, select the main central stem or trunk, then start pruning off the lower side stems, and over a period of time keep cutting out these side branches, until the branching starts at approximately 1.8m (6ft). Prune downward-pointing branches, so that the lower foliage is a nice level line. To help this main trunk grow as straight as possible, one or two 2.5m (10ft) wooden or metal stakes should be forced into the ground right next to the trunk, then tied to the trunk at three or four points along their length.

4. Even out the shape of a plant (particularly shrubs and vines) by pruning the ends of branches that stick out unevenly. This will give the plant a lush compact appearance.

5. To produce a multi-trunk tree or large shrub, select 2-4 main branches, as close to the ground as possible, which will produce an interesting spreading effect. Cut the other main branches off at their base, then prune the small branchlets off the lower part of the remaining main branches. As the plant

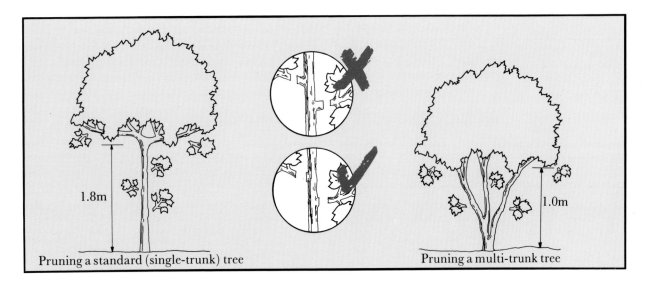

Pruning a standard (single-trunk) tree   Pruning a multi-trunk tree

grows, keep pruning the lower branchlets off, so that the trunks are bare up to 1 or 1.5m (3-5ft). In some weaker-stemmed plants, such as *Lagerstroemia indica* (Crape Myrtle) and *Tecoma stans*, 1.5-2m (5-7ft) stakes may be required to support the trunks in the proper direction.

6. Vines should be pruned so that stems are generally of equal length, to avoid that leggy, rangy look. Pruning just above outward-pointing branches will also help to train them to spread laterally.

When to prune

Light pruning to shape a plant or remove dead twigs can be done all year. However, heavy pruning, where you are cutting main branches or large diameter branches, should be done in the dormant winter season (December-February). Deciduous trees in particular belong to this category. It is much easier to see their true structural shape when all their leaves have fallen off, so that branches can be cut right back to give the tree better balance. One exception to this rule is the *Albizzia julibbrissin* (Silk Tree). Pruning it while it is deciduous can cause severe dieback, so wait until new growth has started in the spring to do your pruning.

Pruning tools

There are a variety of different tools specially designed for the type of pruning you are doing, and the thickness of the branch to be cut (see illustration on p. 72).

Pruning shears: these are about the size of a pair of kitchen scissors, and are the primary pruning tool. There are two basic types – anvil and shear (hook and blade). Both are equally good. Also available are specialized fruit shears, propagating shears, and flower shears.

Lopping shears (loppers): these are for cutting thicker branches that need more leverage for cutting and for reaching higher up into trees. The 'hook and blade' type are preferred, as the 'hook' portion can hold the branch while cutting. Be sure to get good ones with sturdy shanks and strong handles.

Grass shears: scissor-type shears for cutting grass edges or borders.

Hedge shears (clippers): for clipping the straight edges and rectangular shapes of formal hedges.

71

Pole pruner with pole saws: for very high branches, up to 2.5cm (1in) thick. This consists of a long pole with a pruning saw at the end, plus a cord-operated clipper inside a round hook that fits over a branch.

Pruning saws: these are heavy-toothed saws designed for cutting green wood. There are two types: curved saws which can work in close spaces, and cut on the pull stroke – handy for overhead limbs, and straight (bow) saws – for lower branches where you have space to work – which cut on the push stroke.

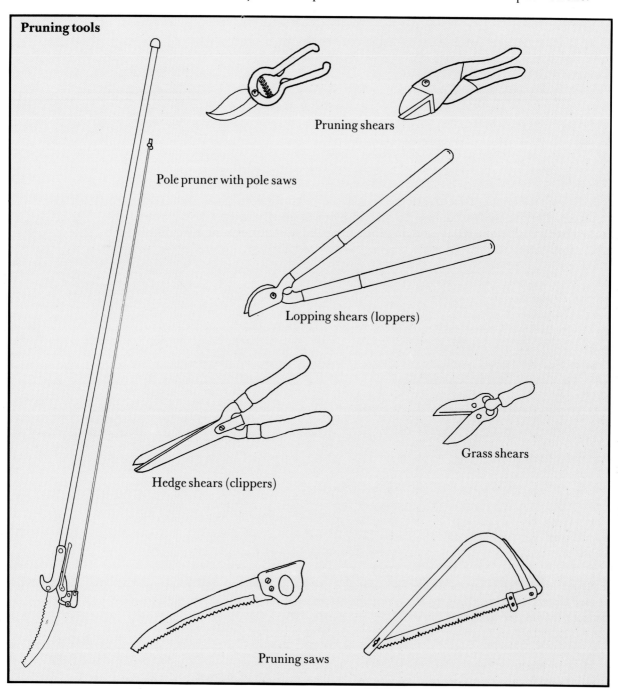

Pruning tools

Pruning shears

Pole pruner with pole saws

Lopping shears (loppers)

Hedge shears (clippers)

Grass shears

Pruning saws

PROPAGATION

PERHAPS THE MOST interesting and rewarding part of gardening is propagation: new life created from a combination of soil, water, and seeds or twigs. The three most common types of propagation are seed, cuttings and division.

Seed

Almost all plants that are grown from seed will get off to a much better start if sown in containers and later transplanted into the ground.

Any container that will hold soil and has a hole or holes in the bottom to drain off water will do well for starting seeds. Clay or plastic pots, cut-down milk cartons or water bottles, and even styrofoam cups can be used, but do not forget to punch holes in the bottom for drainage. If you use plastic nursery flats, or other containers that have held plants, scrub them out first with a powerful cleaner and allow them to dry to avoid 'damping off' (fungus) infection of the soil mix.

If it is available from your local nursery or flower shop, it is best to use a prepared soil mix labelled 'potting soil'. If not, a mix of equal parts of sand, peat moss, and Perlite will do the job. This mix will drain easily, yet still retain the moisture. Fill your container firmly with the mixture up to 1½-2cm (½-1in) from the top. If the mixture is dry, soak it with water, and wait a day or so before planting. Very fine seeds can be scattered over the surface, then covered with a thin layer of sand or potting soil. Larger seeds can be planted in shallow furrows or poked in individually, and covered with soil to a depth roughly twice the seed diameter. Follow the directions on the individual seed packets. Then water immediately with a fine spray, soaking the soil all the way through, or lower into a tub or sink containing about 5cm (2in) of water, and allow to sit for half an hour.

Place the container in a warm shaded spot where it will get just a little light, preferably indoors. Keep moist but not wet. When the first seedlings have developed their second set of true leaves (what appears to be the first set of leaves is actually part of the seed's cotyledon), it is time to transplant or thin them out. If many more plants have sprouted than you can use, remove enough plants to leave those remaining 3-5cm (1-2in) apart. Grow these for 3 to 4 weeks until they reach 6-10cm (2½-4in) high, then carefully lift them out, keeping the soil around each root system, and transplant into the ground. However, if you want to keep most of the seedlings, they will have to be transplanted into larger containers, for further growth before planting into your garden.

For this first transplanting, loosen the soil around the seedling plant and carefully lift it out, using a kitchen fork so as not to lose the roots and surrounding soil. Place the seedling's roots and soil in the new container, which should be filled with moist potting soil. Firm the soil around the plant. Keep these plants out of direct sunlight for 4-6 days to help avoid transplant shock.

3-6 weeks after this initial transplant, the seedlings will have developed a full root system, reached 10-15cm (5-7in) in height, and should be ready to plant in the ground. During the interim, keep the soil moist but not wet, and, to aid growth, fertilize once with a mild dose of liquid plant food.

Cuttings

Cuttings are really nothing more than living twigs or small sections of a plant's stem. There are three types: *softwood cuttings* should be taken in the spring or early summer while the plant is putting on new growth. These generally are the quickest rooting, and the easiest for a novice to work with. They can be taken from trees, shrubs, vines or ground covers. *Semi-hardwood cuttings* should be taken in the summer or autumn, when the new growth is slowing down and hardening. They should be taken at a point of the stem where it will break, not bend, if bent sharply.

Bougainvillaea is a good example of a plant that roots well from semi-hardwood cuttings, but gives poor results from softwood. *Hardwood cuttings* are those taken from deciduous trees or shrubs during the winter dormant season. They are much more difficult to root than the other two. To take cuttings, cut a stem up to 60cm (24in) back from the tip depending on the type of plant, so that you retain at least four leaf nodes (joints). If you have a long stem, cut it into sections so that you have four nodes per section. Strip the leaves off the two lower nodes. Using a nail or pencil, make small holes in your rooting soil – these should be slightly smaller than the thickness of the stems – then push the cuttings into the holes so that the two nodes with leaves are above the soil, and the two without leaves are in the soil. It is a good idea to cut the leaves in half on each cutting to reduce the water requirements while it is rooting.

The rooting medium (soil mix) most commonly used in the Gulf is one-half peat moss, and one-half Perlite. It is best to ensure the peat moss has been well-shredded before use, so that it will mix well with the Perlite, and absorb water. Finely ground bark is a good substitute for peat moss. Sand can be used, but the results will not be as good.

Before pushing your cuttings into the soil, it is best to dip the lower end of each one into a rooting hormone powder. Rooting will then take place much faster.

If you are propagating a large number of cuttings, it is best to use nursery 'flats' (or trays) to hold your soil medium, accommodating up to 100 cuttings in each flat. Otherwise use a clay pot or a can with holes in the bottom.

Keep the soil moist, but not saturated. Overwatering can produce root rot and wilting. Keep in a well-lit area (inside or outside), but not in direct sunlight. After the cuttings have rooted (this will take from two weeks to three months, depending on the plant), carefully transplant them into small pots, keeping the original soil medium around each rooted cutting. Keep them in shade until new growth is well on its way.

Some of the more popular plants that require propagation from cuttings are bougainvillaea, carissa, clerodendron, ficus, hibiscus, oleander, and thevetia.

Divisions

If you have perennial bedding plants, bulbs, or plants with rhizomes or tubers in your garden, then these can be divided to make new plants. In some cases it makes the plant healthier and more vigorous if you do divide them every two or three years. This is particularly so if plants are crowding each other and competing for the moisture in the soil.

In most areas, the best time to divide plants is in the winter dormant season. In the cooler, higher elevations, divide plants in the autumn or early spring.

To divide the plants, simply push a shovel, spade, trowel, or knife down through the centre of the plant, cutting through the entire root system. Loosen, then lift out that portion of the plant you will be transplanting. Fill the hole with soil, then immediately plant your new division in another hole, and firmly tamp the soil around it. Small perennials may be lifted out of the soil and pulled apart. Bulbs that are perennials should not be divided until flower production has ended, then they should be dug up and the bulbs pulled apart. Replant or store bulbs until the appropriate planting time.

Plants you can propagate by dividing include agapanthus, asparagus ferns, canna lilies, dahlias, gladioli, and fortnight lilies.

GARDEN MAINTENANCE

MAINTAINING A GARDEN is not all that different from maintaining a house – a lot of cleaning, straightening, and picking things up is involved. The big difference is that in the garden you have the advantage of fresh air and sunshine while you are doing it. In the house, you may be rearranging furniture, while in the garden you are transplanting or putting in new plants. In the house, it is a vacuum cleaner, outside, a lawn mower or rake. Most compounds, and some villas, have landscape maintenance service provided. But if you are doing your own, then this section is for you.

Tools for garden maintenance
The key to garden maintanance is to have the right tools for each job. The following is a list of basic tools needed, and the jobs they have been designed to do:

Long-handled round-point shovel: multi-purpose, but mainly for digging holes when planting or transplanting.
Square-point shovel: mixing and moving soil, and cleaning up.
Round-point spade: digging trenches and small holes, or uprooting large weeds.
Hoe: cultivating or mixing soil, and weeding.
Weeding hoe: for digging up smaller weeds and planting ground cover plants.
Hand trowel: planting small plants and working soil.
Cultivator: cultivating soil, weeding.
Bow rake: smoothing, levelling soil, breaking up dirt clods, raking in seed, spreading mulch and cleaning up.
Leaf rake: cleaning up leaves and twigs.

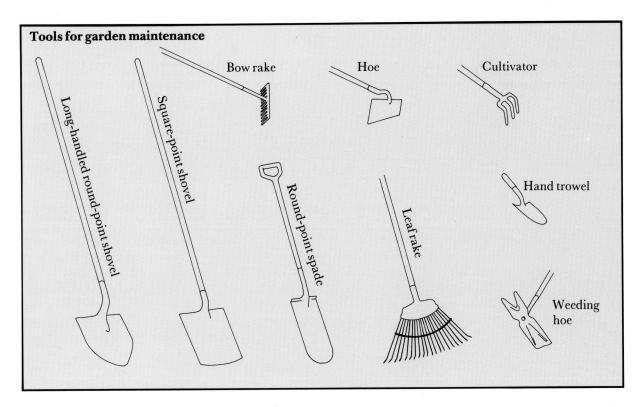

Tools for garden maintenance

Long-handled round-point shovel • Square-point shovel • Bow rake • Hoe • Cultivator • Round-point spade • Leaf rake • Hand trowel • Weeding hoe

Staking, tying

Almost all newly planted standard (single trunk) trees should have stakes next to the trunk. These should be 5cm×5cm (2in×2in) wooden stakes, or 2.5cm (1in) metal stakes, 2.5m (8ft) long, and pushed into the ground 60cm (24in), as close to the trunk of the tree as possible (8-10cm/3-4in). The stake is then tied to the tree using a wire pushed through plastic tubing, a strip of rubber tyre inner tube, or rubber ties which are manufactured for this purpose. Such ties should be applied at 3 or 4 different points, each in a figure-of-eight pattern, so that they strap around both the tree and the stake. The purpose, of course, is to keep the trunk straight. For smaller trees (under 1.5m/5ft high) a shorter, thinner stake can be used, but this will have to be changed when the tree reaches 2m (6ft) or taller.

Multi-trunk trees or large shrubs may have to be staked to give direction to each trunk so that an overall pleasing, spreading shape is achieved.

Some flowering plants or perennials may need staking, particularly after large blooms appear, so as to prevent the narrow stems from drooping or bending. 1m (3ft) wood or bamboo stakes should do the job. Tie fairly loosely with stretchable green vinyl tape, if available, or with string. This same type of tape should be used when tying vines to trellises or arbors.

Cleaning up

A neat garden is a healthy, more pleasing one. Piles of dead leaves, twigs, wood, and trash are breeding grounds for insects, soil pests, and other injurious creatures. Get into the habit of going out into your garden once or twice a week with pruning shears, a hand trowel, tying material, and a bucket or bag. Prune out dead twigs, old flowers, unwanted seed pods, and leggy branches. Remove weeds and pick up dead leaves and trash. Put it all in your handy bucket, and, when finished, dump it in the rubbish bin. This 15-30 minute weekly exercise will keep your garden looking neat, make you aware if watering, fertilizing, or pest problems arise, and avoid major cleaning or weeding chores later on.

SECTION FOUR
THE
PLANT ENCYCLOPEDIA

Introduction

In this section, individual plants are described by their growth habit, type of foliage, flowers, use in a garden or landscape, method of propagation, and, in cases where it is a recurring problem, susceptibility to pests or diseases.

Each plant is listed alphabetically by its Latin genus name of which the initial letter is capitalized, then its species name, followed by its common English name in parentheses. Where it is known, the Arabic name is also given. The common names of plants are also listed alphabetically, with a cross reference to the Latin botanical name. It is helpful to learn the botanical names of plants, since in many nurseries the common names will not be known.

All measurements are approximations only.

The climatic zones listed for each species are also, of necessity, approximations. The survival of a plant in your area can be affected by unusual weather patterns, such as an abnormally hot summer or unusually cold winter. Where it is known, the salt-tolerance of a species is expressed in parts per million (ppm) of total dissolved salts in irrigation water. Most plants listed have been observed growing in the Middle East by the author, but there are also species shown that are known to grow in similar climatic areas, for example the deserts of the southwestern United States and Australia, that are educated guesses. They should do well here, but at the time of writing have not been seen in the Middle East.

The Middle Eastern climate can make it difficult to predict when and for how long some plants will flower (see pp. 39-40). For this reason some entries in the plant encyclopedia do not have their flowering seasons defined.

The plant encyclopedia is primarily devoted to plants commonly used in landscaping and gardening in the Middle East. There are comparatively few native plants listed.

A

Acacia

Evergreen shrubs and trees, found in warm, temperate or arid regions throughout the world. The majority of the species are native to Australia. Most of those that grow in desert areas have finely divided foliage with small leaflets (bipinnate), and all have yellow flowers.

The acacia can be pruned as a shrub or as a tree. Remove the terminal stem and it grows as a shrub: remove the lower side branches and it will become tree-like. Tree types will require staking until the main stem is self-supporting.

They are generally drought-tolerant. If watered deeply, but infrequently, surface rooting will be discouraged and the deeper root system will give better anchorage in the soil. Much of the water and soil in the Arabian peninsula is salty and alkaline, and will produce chlorosis (yellowing of the leaves) in acacias. Treat with chelated iron. Propagate from seed.

A. arabica

(Arabian Acacia)
Arabic: *Anber*
All zones. Native to the Arabian peninsula. Very drought-tolerant, existing in the Nejd and Rub Al Khali areas on 5-10cm (2-4in) of rain per year, and will tolerate brackish water up to 8,000 ppm of salt. A large shrub or small tree reaching 5m (17ft), in landscape situations it needs frequent pruning (every two months) to achieve a pleasing, symmetrical shape. Tends to get leggy and rangy when unpruned. 16-20, fine, 1cm-long (0.4in) leaflets are carried on each leaf that branches out from the side branches, with long, 2-3cm (1in) thorns. The small, yellow, fluffy, ball-like spring flowers are not as showy as other acacias. In the desert it provides nourishment for camels, which have the unique ability to place their mouths over the stem and strip off the foliage without being punctured by the thorns.

A. baileyana

(Bailey Acacia)
Zones 1,3,5,7. The cut flowers are sold as 'mimosa'. Coastal zones. Perhaps the most beautiful of all the acacias. Grows to 6-8m (20-26ft), a round-headed tree with finely cut, blue-grey foliage. Profuse clusters of bright yellow flowers are borne in January and February. Attractive as a multi-trunk tree.

A. cyanophylla

(Blue Leaf Wattle)
Zones 1,3,5,7. Salt-tolerant to 5,000 ppm. This

(above) *Acacia arabica* (Arabian Acacia), (left) *Acacia baileyana* (Bailey Acacia)

is a multi-trunk, round-headed, small tree or large shrub reaching 6m×4m (20ft×13ft). It has narrow, attractive foliage and bears yellow-orange balls in early spring.

A. decurrens

(Green Wattle)
Zones 1,3,5,7. Salt-tolerant to 6,000 ppm or more. This 12-15m (40-50ft) tree has finely cut foliage and yellow flower clusters in spring.

A. farnesiana

(Sweet Acacia)
All zones. Salt-tolerant to 10,000 ppm or more. This is a deciduous multi-trunk tree with very fine green foliage and thorny branches. Yellow, fragrant balls are borne from January to April. A good tree for screening or border planting.

A. ongerop

All zones. Tolerates salt up to 7,000 ppm. This is a drought-tolerant, wide-spreading, low-growing ground cover. 50-70cm (20-30in) high and 5-6m (17-20ft) spread. The long, narrow leaves are greenish-grey. The early spring flowers are small, puffy, yellow balls. Propagate from cuttings.

Acacia-Algerian Ivy

Albizzia lebbeck
(Mother's Tongue)

A. saligna
(Willow Acacia).
Zones 1,3,5,7. This very fast-growing, graceful, weeping tree reaches 6m (20ft) high and 8m (27ft) spread. It is most handsome as a multi-trunk tree, but is often used as a large screening shrub. The long, narrow, dark green leaves, up to 20cm (8in) in length, have a somewhat twisting habit. Clusters of large, yellow, showy flowers are borne in mid-spring. In its native Australia *Acacia saligna* is part of the Koala Bear's diet. Propagate from seed.

Adam's Needle: see *Yucca filamentosa*

Aden Apple: see *Thespesia*

Adenanthera pavoniana
(Red Sandalwood Tree)
Zones 1,3,5,7. Native to India. A semi-deciduous tree reaching 9m (30ft). This is a bipinnate tree, whose leaves up to 45cm (18in) long, have 3-5cm (1-2in) leaflets. The whitish-yellow spring flowers are followed by sickle-shaped seed pods. Growth can be ungainly if pruning is not regular. Propagate from seeds that have been presoaked in hot water.

African Daisy, Trailing: see *Osteospermum*

African Sumac: see *Rhus*

Agapanthus
(Lily of the Nile)
Zones 1,5,7. These evergreen perennials, which reach 60cm (24in) high have long, narrow, arching leaves. They should be grown on the north or east side of a house or wall, or in shade. They do not like full summer sun. This is a good plant for small borders.

A. africanus
The clumps of leaves are 50-60cm (20-24in) high and wide. Tall flower stalks carry large, round, blue or white flower clusters on top in summer. Propagate from seed or by division.

A. 'Peter Pan'
This is a dwarf hybrid with thinner leaves; the clumps are 30-40cm (12-16in) high and wide. Profuse blooms are borne on 35-40cm (14-16in) stalks. A white variety is also available.

Agave americana
(Century Plant)
Zones 1,3,5,6,7. Salt-tolerant to 2,000 ppm. A giant succulent with large clumps of thick, 6m-long (20ft) leaves. The leaves have barbed edges and a sharp pointed tip. The clumps are up to 3m (10ft) wide. 10-12-year-old plants will grow a 6-9m (20-30ft) branching flower stalk. Soft green-yellow flowers are borne in summer and autumn. Propagate from seed.

Ajuga reptans
(Carpet Bugle)
All zones. Sun or shade. This is a low-growing ground cover that spreads by runners. Small, rounded, blue flowers are borne on short stalks in spring. The leaves are 5-10cm (2-4in) long; some hybrid varieties have bronze-coloured foliage.

Albizzia
Deciduous and semi-deciduous, wide-spreading shade trees. All zones. Propagate from seed.

A. julibrissin
(Silk Tree, Mimosa)
Umbrella-shaped, with greater spread than height, this tree looks best as a multi-trunk. The finely divided leaflets are 1-2cm (1in) long; pink, fluffy summer flowers blossom above the foliage, making it a tree best viewed from above, and therefore useful in courtyards or patios. Long seed pods are carried in the autumn. Prune it to shape in spring, 2-3 weeks after new growth appears, and in late summer. Pruning while deciduous in the winter can cause severe dieback.

A. lebbeck
(Mother's Tongue)
Arabic: *Abkh*
Semi-deciduous. Salt-tolerant to 3,000-4,000 ppm. This is a large, round-headed shade tree reaching a height of 15m (50ft) which can get leggy and rangy-looking if not pruned once or twice a year. The leaflets are larger than those of *A. julibrissin*, but they share the same single-edged, oval shape. The 8cm (3in), white, fluffy, brush-like summer flowers are more evident in coastal areas. It is used as a street tree in many cities.

Algerian Ivy: *see Hedera*

Aloe-Angel's Trumpet

Aloe
Hardy succulents of the Lily family. Zones 1,3,5,7. Native to South Africa. Salt-tolerant to 3,000 ppm. The clumps of leaves are long, narrow and fleshy, with orange, red, or yellow flowers. Aloes range from tree size down to 30cm (1ft) shrublets. Propagate from seed.

A. arborescens
(Tree Aloe)
The grey-green, tooth-edged leaves form clumps. The branching stems may reach 6m (20ft) and clusters of spiky, tapering, 12cm-long (5in), red to yellow flowers bloom on tall stalks in winter. Tolerates shade.

A. saponaria
This aloe's spread is greater than its height. The thick, broad, green leaves have white spots. The 50cm-long (20in), branching, orange-pink flower clusters bloom in winter.

A. variegata
(Tiger Aloe)
The 30cm-high (12in) rosettes of triangular leaves are variegated green and white. Reddish-pink flower clusters appear intermittently throughout the year.

A. vera
(Medicine Plant)
The juice from the narrow, fleshy, spiny leaves is said to improve the complexion and to have curative medicinal powers. This is a good container plant.

Alternanthera versicolor
Zones 1,3,5,7. Native to Brazil. This is a low-growing, clumping ground cover, with striking, deep red to green foliage. The leaves are 2-3cm (1in) long. It makes an excellent border plant next to lawns and walkways. Insignificant flowers. Propagate from cuttings or by division.

Althea rosea
(Hollyhock)
Biennial. All zones. Salt-tolerant to 7,000 ppm. This is a tall, rangy plant reaching a height of 2.5m (8ft) with 10-15cm (4-6in), lobed, rough, heart-shaped leaves. Large, multi-coloured, single or double flower spikes appear in late spring and summer. The leaves are susceptible to rust. Propagate from seed.

Aloe arborescens (Tree Aloe)

Alyssum, Sweet: see *Lobularia*

Amaranthus tricolor
(Joseph's Coat)
Annual. All zones. This is a 1.5m (3ft) shrub, with wide, 12cm (5in), reddish-green leaves. Small clusters of red flowers are borne. Propagate from seed.

Amaryllis belladonna
(Belladonna Lily)
Bulb. All zones. Salt- and drought-tolerant. The tall, straplike leaves grow to a height of 1m (3ft) in clumps 60-70cm (24-28in) wide. Pink, 10cm (4in), trumpet-shaped flowers are borne on 80cm (32in), reddish-brown stalks in late summer and autumn.

Anethum graveolens
(Dill)
Annual herb. All zones. This herb can grow up to 1.5m (5ft) high, with feathery leaves, 15cm-wide (6in) and umbrella-shaped clusters of small yellow flowers. The leaves and seeds are fragrant: the seeds are used to make vinegar, whilst fresh leaves are used in salads, and dried leaves for flavouring in cooking.

Angel's Trumpet: see *Datura*

81

Anise-Athel Tree

Asparagus sprengeri
(Asparagus Fern)

Anise: see *Pimpinella*

Anthemis nobilis
(Chamomile)
All zones. This can be a lawn substitute for small areas. The light green, fine-textured foliage spreads to form a thick carpet, giving off fragrance when crushed or stepped upon. Plant 30cm (12in) apart. Yellow, button-like or daisy flowers appear in summer. The dried flower heads can be used to make chamomile tea. Propagate from seed or by division.

Antigonon leptotus
(Coral Vine)
All zones. Semi-deciduous. Native to Mexico. This very fast-growing vine climbs by tendrils to 10-12m (33-40ft). The dark green, 10cm-long (4in) leaves are arrow-shaped. Small pink flowers are borne on long, trailing sprays in summer and autumn. This is a sun-loving plant, which is useful for arbors or open pavilions. It needs frequent pruning to keep it lush. Propagate from cuttings.

Antirrhinum majus
(Snapdragon)
This perennial is usually grown as an annual or biennial. All zones. The many different varieties vary in height from 30-120cm (12-48in); dwarf forms reach 15-20cm (6-8in). It flowers profusely in spring and summer; many different colours are available. The flowers are tubular and jaw-like, and grow on vertical spikes; the dark green leaves are 8cm (3in) long. This is an excellent border plant. Propagate from seed.

Apple: see **Fruit Trees, Deciduous**

Arabian Acacia: see *Acacia*

Arabian Jasmine: see *Jasminum*

Arctotheca calendula
(Cape Weed)
Zones 1,3,5,7. This perennial ground cover is similar to the trailing Gazania. Yellow daisy-like flowers are borne from spring until the autumn. The narrow foliage is grey-green. It does best if it is planted where it will receive morning or winter sun, but shade in summer. Propagate from seed.

Argyreia campanulata
Zones 1,3,5,7. Native to India and Malaysia. This is a wild, rangy shrub reaching up to 3m (10ft), with many stems at its base. The dark green, wedge-shaped leaves have grey undersides. The pinkish-lilac flowers are short-lived. It can be used to make a spreading, informal hedge. Propagate from seed or cuttings.

Artemesia
Drought-resistant shrubs and perennials. All zones. Propagate from seed or by division.

A. absinthum
(Wormwood)
This is a woody shrub reaching 1m (3ft) high with finely divided grey leaves. Very small yellow flowers appear in spring. It needs pruning to be attractive. The dried leaves are used for medicinal purposes, and for seasoning.

A. dracunculus
(French Tarragon)
This is a very fragrant perennial, reaching a height of 50cm (20in). It spreads by means of creeping rhizomes. The narrow, dark green leaves are shiny. Clusters of greenish-white flowers are borne in spring. The leaves (fresh or dried) are used to season fish or omelettes, or in salads.

Arundo donax
(Giant Reed)
All zones. The bamboo-like, woody stems reach 6m (20ft) in height, with 50cm-long (20in), narrow leaves. It requires a lot of space and frequent pruning to avoid being messy.

Ash: see *Fraxinus*

Asparagus sprengeri
(Asparagus Fern)
All zones. This is a versatile plant, which will tolerate full sun, or grow indoors near a window. The long, green, cascading stems have short, needle-like foliage. It can be used as a ground cover or as a spreading border shrub and is also excellent as a container plant, and in hanging baskets. The insignificant, tiny white flowers are followed by whitish berries. This is a useful shade plant. Propagate from seed or by division.

Athel Tree: see *Tamarix*

Atriplex-Azederacha

Atriplex

Evergreen shrubs. Drought-tolerant, and salt-tolerant to 5,000-8,000 ppm. These are excellent desert plants, usually grown for their silver-grey foliage. Flowers, if any, are insignificant. Propagate from seed or cuttings.

A. glauca

Zones 1,3,5,7. A round-headed bush reaching 1m (3ft) high. The 8cm (3in) leaves are blueish-grey.

A. halimus

(Mediterranean Salt Bush)
Zones 1,3,5,7. Native to Southern Europe. This is a round-headed, dense shrub which reaches up to 2cm (6ft) high. It can be used for clipped formal hedges. The round, silver-grey leaves are 5cm (2in) in diameter. It is a deep-rooted plant, which is useful for sand stablization.

A. semibaccata

(Australian Salt Bush)
All zones. This small-leafed, grey-green ground cover grows up to 30cm (1ft) high and 2m (6ft) wide. It is deep-rooted and so useful for sand stablization.

Australian Willow: see *Geijera*

Azederacha indica

(Neem Tree)
Arabic: *Neem*
Evergreen tree. Zones 1,5. Salt-tolerant to at least 2,000 ppm. This round-headed, somewhat open-branched tree reaches a height of 10m (33ft). It is widely used as a street tree in Jiddah, Saudi Arabia. The bipinnate leaves are divided into 8-12 pairs of 5cm-long (2in), deep green, pointed leaflets with toothed edges. Pale white flowers are borne in clusters in summer. The berry-like fruits and the leaves are used for medicinal purposes. Propagate from seed.

(above) *Atriplex halimus* (Mediterranean Salt Bush), (left) *Azederacha indica* (Neem Tree)

Bailey Acacia-Bottle Tree

B

Bauhinia variegata
(Purple Orchid Tree)

Bailey Acacia: see *Acacia*

Balm of Gilead: see *Populus*

Banana: see *Musa*

Banyan, Weeping Chinese: see *Ficus*

Barbados Pride: see *Poinciana*

Basil: see *Ocimum*

Bauhinia
These evergreen or deciduous trees and shrubs
have twin-lobed leaves like green butterflies.
Colourful, orchid-like flowers appear in spring.
Propagate from seed or cuttings.

B. galpini
(Red Bauhinia)
Zones 1,3,5,7. Native to South Africa. This
makes a 4m (13ft) shrub or multi-trunk tree.
The deep red to orange, 10cm (4in) flowers
bloom best in coastal areas. It needs regular
pruning to prevent it from sprawling.

B. variegata
(Purple Orchid Tree)
All zones. Semi-deciduous. Native to India and
China. The spectacular, pink or purple, 6-7cm-
long (2-3in) spring flowers are more profuse in
coastal areas. Best as a multi-trunk tree.

Beefwood: see *Casuarina*

Belladonna Lily: see *Amaryllis*

Bermuda Grass: see *Cynadon dactylon*

Bird of Paradise Bush: see *Poinciana*

Black Locust: see *Robinia*

Blue Fescue: see *Festuca*

Blue Palo Verde: see *Cercidium*

Boswellia carterii
(Frankincense)
Zone 7. A drought-resistant, small evergreen
tree or large shrub reaching 3m (10ft). This is a
craggy and picturesque plant with ash-coloured
branches, red bark, and tiny, greenish-blue
leaves. The source of a famous Middle Eastern
incense, which was found in Tutankhamun's
tomb. The fragrant gum-resin is allowed to
harden into pearly-white beads on the tree.
After a few weeks it is harvested and dried in
caves. Propagate from seed.

Bottlebrush: see *Callistemon*

Bottle Tree: see *Brachichyton*

Bougainvillaea-Button Mangrove

Bougainvillaea spectabilis

Arabic: *Jahanamiyeh*

All zones. Evergreen vines and shrubby ground covers. Salt tolerant to 2,000 ppm. This is one of the most widely grown and spectacular flowering plants on the Arabian peninsula. It will lose its leaves and experience dieback if exposed to temperatures below 28°F, but, after the first year, will grow back in the spring. Bougainvillaea will bloom 8-12 months of the year.

Bougainvillaea's vibrant colours come not from the inconspicuous flowers, but from the three large bracts that surround them. This is a vigorous plant that likes full sun, and provides a dense cover of 4-7cm (1-2in), mid-green leaves. It can be readily pruned to cover a wall or trellis. The thorny stems make it prudent to wear gloves when handling.

Take great care when planting bougain-villaea, as the roots are most sensitive, and do not knit the soil into a tight root ball. If the root ball breaks or crumbles, exposing the roots, the plant will die.

Water normally while the plants are growing fast in the spring, then cut back watering temporarily when flowers appear, and you will get a greater abundance of flowers. Fertilize in early spring and early summer with a complete fertilizer. Prune heavily in early spring to re-establish the plant shape and to produce more flowering wood. Cut away long, leggy stems throughout the year to maintain a symmetrical shape. Propagate by cuttings.

There are numerous varieties that thrive in the Middle East, and some of the better ones are shown below. Those listed below are vines, except where specified as shrubs or ground covers.

'Barbara Karst': profuse, bright red in full sun, turns a blueish crimson when shaded. One of the longest-blooming varieties.
'Brasiliensis': large masses of vibrant purple.
'California Gold': deeper green leaves with a pale yellow-gold bloom.
'Crimson Jewel': one of the best to use as a shrub, but also effective as a ground cover. Luxurious dark green leaves and brilliant red flowers.
'Hawaii': good as ground cover or as a mounding shrub. Interesting, variegated green and yellow leaves with red flowers.
'Jamaica White': a frosty white bloom with greenish veins.

A unique *Bougainvillaea*, with red and white flowers on the same plant

'La Jolla': perhaps the most widely known of the bright reds.
'Orange King': bronze-orange: seen frequently in Riyadh.
'Pink Tiara': delicate pink to rose colour.
'San Diego Red': one of the old, reliable, vigorous reds.
'Temple Fire': a bronze-red bush form.

Brachichyton (Sterculia) populneum

(Bottle Tree)

Zones 1,3,5,7. The common name is derived from the broad-based trunk which tapers rapidly. The attractive, semi-pyramidal shape reaches up to 15m (50ft) high and 8m (26ft) wide. The shimmering, lobed leaves have prominent white veins. Small, bell-shaped white flowers are borne in mid-spring, followed by scimitar-shaped brown fruits. Propagate from cuttings or seed.

Brazilian Skyflower: see *Duranta*

Brooms: see *Cytisus*

Bunny Ears: see *Cactus*

Button Mangrove: see *Conocarpus*

Cactus-Callistemon

C

Callistemon viminalis
(Weeping
Bottlebrush)

Cactus
The genus contains a wide range of slow-growing, thorny, succulent plants, ranging from tree size to cup size. Native to the Americas. Many are native to tropical rain forest areas, and will not take the dry desert heat. However, they make useful house plants. Propagate from seed.

Listed below are some of those that will tolerate the Middle Eastern environment, and can be used to create a desert garden.

Echinocactus
(Barrel Cactus)
Zones 1,3,5,7. This is a cylindrical cactus with notable, variegated ribs. The yellow thorns are up to 7cm (3in) long. Yellow, 5cm-long (2in) flowers appear in spring.

Espostoa lanata
(Old Man Cactus)
Zones 1,3,5,7. This columnar cactus reaches 4m (13ft), branching when 5-6 years old. Its name derives from the white, hairlike strands that hang from the top, partially covering the brown, bristly, 5cm-long (2in) thorns. Pink, tubular flowers are borne in spring.

Ferocactus
All zones. Native to south-west United States. This globe-shaped to cylindrical cactus is ribbed and spiny. Yellow-orange flowers are borne in spring.

Lemaireocereus thurberi
(Organpipe cactus)
Zones 1,3,5,7. This is a tree-like, columnar cactus, branching from the base. The ribbed green and grey-green stems have short, black spines. The 8cm-long (3in), whitish-purple flowers bloom at night. They are followed by small, edible, green fruit with red pulp.

Opuntia ficus-indica
(Indian Fig Cactus)
All zones. This rangy, shrubby cactus grows up to 5m (17ft) high, with woody trunks, and flat smooth pads or joints 30-50cm (18-20in) long. It has few thorns, but clusters of small bristles. The large yellow flowers are followed by large, red or yellow, edible fruit.

O. microdasys
(Bunny Ears)
Zones 1,3,5,7. This is a fast-growing, wide-spreading, bushy cactus reaching 60cm (24in) high and 1.5m (5ft) wide. The round, flat, thin pads are up to 15cm (6in) long, with tufts of golden bristles that give a polka-dot effect. New pads grow in layers on top of larger, older ones.

Caesalpinia: see **Poinciana**

Cajeput Tree: see **Melaleuca**

Calendula officinalis
(Pot Marigold)
Annual or short-lived perennial. All zones. Bright yellow or orange double flowers are borne for 9 or 10 months of the year. The tongue-shaped, light green leaves are 20cm (8in) long. It is good for borders or drifts of flowers in a free-form landscape. Propagate from seed.

California Pepper: see **Schinus**

Callistemon
(Bottlebrush)
Evergreen trees and shrubs. All zones but 6. Native to Australia. Salt-tolerant to 2,500 ppm. Callistemon are characterised by narrow stemless leaves and colourful, round or cylindrical summer-flowering blooms, from whose red, thread-like stamens the common name is derived. The brown, bead-like seeds grow out of woody, cone-like capsules. Propagate from seed or cuttings.

C. citrinus (lanceolatus)
(Lemon Bottlebrush)
This is a dense shrub, reaching 4m (13ft) which can easily be pruned and trained as an attractive, multi-trunk tree. The 6-8cm (2-3in) narrow leaves are copper-coloured in new growth. This is a good plant for screening or for providing a garden highlight.

C. viminalis
(Weeping Bottlebrush)
This is a small tree reaching 8m (27ft) with arching, pendulous branches. It has longer leaves than *C. citrinus*. It blooms from early spring until autumn. New growth tends to be concentrated at the ends of the branches, and so regular pruning is needed to keep the tree dense and shapely. This is an attractive tree which can be planted in groups to create a woodland effect.

Calotropis-Carolina Jasmine

Calotropis procera
(Faftan Calotrope)
All zones. Salt-tolerant to 6,000 ppm. A native of
North Africa, it grows wild in the desert areas.
This is a large evergreen shrub reaching 3.5m
(12ft). The light green, hairy, rounded leaves
angle out from branches emanating from the
base. The star-shaped, purple flowers bloom in
the spring and are followed by kidney-shaped,
green fruits. Propagate from seed or cuttings.

Camphor Tree: see *Cinnamomum*

Candytuft: see *Iberis*

Canna
Lily-type plant with a tuberous rootstock. All
zones. The 50cm-long (20in) and 10cm-wide
(4in), rich green leaves sometimes turn a bronze
colour. The large flowers are borne in spring and
summer on 1m (3ft) stalks in a wide range of
colours, through white to yellow to red. It is
suitable for tall borders or as a container plant.
Flower stalks should be cut out after the bloom
fades. When the leaves get ragged, cut the plant
to the ground, and it will grow afresh. Propagate
by division.

Cape Plumbago: see *Plumbago*

Cape Weed: see *Arctotheca*

Caraway: see *Carum*

Carissa grandiflora
(Natal Plum)
Zones 1,3,5,7. Native to South Africa. This is a
strong, upright, rounded shrub reaching up to
2m (6ft) high. The dark green, leathery, 7cm-
long (3in) leaves are oval: and 3cm (2in) spines
are borne along the branches. White, fragrant,
star-like flowers appear from spring to autumn,
followed by reddish-orange, small, plum-
shaped, edible fruit. Its density makes it an
excellent screen. Propagate from cuttings.

C. grandiflora
('Boxwood Beauty')
This is a very compact variety reaching 60cm
(2ft), with smaller leaves, and thornier. It can
be used as a clipped, formal border.

C. grandiflora
('Green Carpet')
This is an excellent, wide-spreading ground
cover, reaching 40cm (16in) high and 1m (3ft)

(top) *Calotropis procera*
(Faftan Calotrope),
(above) *Carissa
grandiflora* 'Green
Carpet', (left)
Callistemon citrinus
(Lemon Bottlebrush)

wide. The smaller leaves are half the size of
those of *C. grandiflora*.

Carnation: see *Dianthus*

Carob: see *Ceratonia*

Carolina Jasmine: see *Gelsemium*

Carpet Bugle-Cedrus

Catharanthus rosea
(Madagascar
Periwinkle)

Carpet Bugle: see *Ajuga*

Carpobratus: see **Ice Plant**

Carum carvi
(Caraway)
Biennial herb. This is a mounded, 40cm-high
(16in) plant with lacy, carrot-like leaves. White,
umbrella-shaped flowers are borne the second
year, with seeds in the centre. The plant dies
after the seeds ripen in the summer. Sow seeds in
the spring or autumn. The dried seeds are used
for flavouring pickles, vegetables, breads and
rolls.

Cassia
A wide range of bipinnate evergreen or
deciduous trees and shrubs. Some are tropical,
others are desert species. All have showy yellow
or golden flowers, and bloom erratically
throughout the year. Propagate from seed.

C. didymobotrya (nairobensis)
Zones 1,5 (needs summer shade in zone 3).
Native to East Africa. A leggy, rangy shrub
reaching 3m (10ft). The 5cm-long (2in) leaflets
are carried on 30cm (12in) leaves. The 4cm

(1½in) yellow flowers are carried in dense
clusters.

C. excelsa
(Crown of Gold Tree)
Zones 1,3,5. Native to Argentina. A fast grower
reaching a height of 8-9m (27-30ft). Each leaf
consists of 10-12 pairs of 2-3cm-long (9in)
leaflets. The 30-40cm (12-16in) clusters of
large golden flowers are carried in summer and
autumn. It likes a lot of water, and should be
pruned back heavily after the flowers drop.

C. nodosa
Zones 1,3,5,7. An attractive, somewhat
compact shrub reaching 2m (6½ft). Small
clusters of yellow flowers bloom profusely from
late spring to autumn.

Castor Bean: see *Ricinus*

Casuarina equisitifolia (cunninghamia)
(Beefwood)
Two separate, but almost identical, species. All
zones. Extremely salt-tolerant to 20,000 ppm.
Native to Australia. The long, thin-jointed,
grey-green branches have insignificant leaves,
making them pine-like in appearance. The fruit
is somewhat cone-like, but they are not conifers.
Their height (up to 20m/65ft) makes them good
trees for windbreaks. The foliage is similar to
Tamarisk, but straighter, with a more upright
growth habit. Propagate from seed or cuttings.

Catharanthus rosea, also Vinca rosea
(Madagascar Periwinkle)
Perennial, but usually grown as an annual. All
zones. Use as a ground cover or as a small,
rounded shrub. The profuse flowering of white
to rose pink, 5cm (2in) blossoms continues
almost all year. This is a very popular plant for
street and roadside plantings. It is subject to
chlorosis: treat with iron chelate. Propagate
from seed.

Cat's Claw Vine: see *Doxantha*

Cedar of Lebanon: see *Cedrus libani*

Cedar, Salt: see *Tamarix*

Cedrus libani
(Cedar of Lebanon)
All zones, but best in 2,4 and 7. Native to
Lebanon and Syria: the National Tree of
Lebanon. This is a tall conifer reaching 25m

(85ft), but slow growing, reaching only 4m (13ft) in 12 years. When young it has a narrow pyramid shape, with short, bright green needles: mature trees have a more spreading, majestic shape with blueish-green foliage. It requires deep, infrequent watering. Propagate from seed or cuttings.

Celosia
(Cockscomb, Plumosa)
All zones. This brilliant-flowered annual has two types of flowers: fan-like crested cockscombs, and plume-like clusters. Both are available in red, pink, orange, purple or gold. Varieties range in size from 1m (3ft) down to attractive dwarfs. The leaves are narrow and 5cm (2in) long. Their bright colours make them good as bedding plants or as cut flowers, and (dried) in flower arrangements.

Century Plant: see *Agave*

Ceratonia siliqua
(Carob)
Arabic: *Kharoub*
Evergreen tree. All zones. Slow growing to 15m × 15m (50ft × 50ft). If unpruned it will look like a very large shrub. Pruned, it is equally attractive as a standard or as a multi-trunk tree. The 5cm-long (2in) leaflets are shaped like a rounded square with rippled edges. Small, red, 2cm (1in), circular flowers are borne in spring. The flowers of the male tree give off a strong pungent odour for 3 or 4 weeks in spring. The female tree has many, 30cm-long (12in), dark brown seed pods which are produced in the summer and can be a litter problem. The pods can be ground to produce a sweet chocolate substitute. Over-frequent watering can produce crown root rot. Propagate from cuttings.

Cercidium floridum
(Blue Palo Verde)
Deciduous tree. All zones. This fast-growing tree is similar to *Parkinsonia aculeta* (see p. 119), but with silver-blue foliage and spiny branches. Profuse 10cm (4in) clusters of bright yellow flowers are borne in early spring. Propagate from seed.

Cestrum nocturnum
(Night-blooming Jasmine)
Zones 1,3,5,7. Native to the West Indies. This evergreen shrub reaches 3m (10ft) high with 10-20cm-long (4-8in) leaves. The creamy white, summer flowers are followed by white berries.

Powerful fragrance at night. It is happiest if positioned to receive winter sun and summer shade, or on the east side of the house for morning sun. It will get rangy without regular pruning, and should be cut back heavily after flowering. Propagate from cuttings.

Chamaerops humilis
(Mediterranean Fan Palm)
All zones. This slow-growing palm reaches 6m (20ft) high with fronds similar to the Washingtonia palm (see p. 136) but smaller and with a slightly blueish tinge. Offsets are produced from the base. It makes an attractive container plant. Propagate from seed or by division.

Chamomile: see *Anthemis*

Chaste Tree: see *Vitex*

Chilopsis linearis
(Desert Willow)
All zones. Native to south-west USA. Salt-tolerant to at least 3,000 ppm. This is a semi-deciduous large shrub or small tree reaching 8m (27ft). It is open-headed, with shaggy, brown-grey bark, and long, narrow, 10cm-long (4in) leaves. Trumpet-shaped, pinkish-white flowers with purple markings are borne in spring. Propagate from seed or cuttings.

China Berry: see *Melia*

Chinese Flame Tree: see *Koelruteria*

Chives
This relation of the onion grows in hollow-leaved, grass-like clumps, reaching 40-50cm (16-20in) in height. Lavender-coloured, clover-like flowers are borne in spring. This makes a good plant for the border or the herb garden. Chopped chives can be used with salads, cream cheese, egg dishes, and with sour cream in baked potatoes. Propagate from seed or by division.

Chorisia speciosa
(Floss Silk Tree)
Zones 1,5. Native to Brazil. This semi-deciduous tree reaches a height of 12-15m (40-50ft). It is a fairly fast grower, achieving c.1m (3ft) per year. When young, the tree tends to be narrow, but the crown widens after 5-6 years. The light green, fan-like leaves have 5-7 leaflets. The thick, tapering, green trunk, which has short, heavy spines, turns greyer as it matures.

Chrysanthemum-Cistus

conditions by experienced professionals, but by following the advice below, you may get your plants to flower 2-4 times a year.

Chrysanthemums need more organic material in the soil (30-40%) than most other plants. Apply a complete fertilizer 2 or 3 times during the growing season, but cease applications after the flower buds appear. Pinch off the tip growth when planting, then continue pinching terminal buds during the summer, and also overcrowded flower buds during flowering. Protect the plant from the full afternoon sun during the hottest months. When propagating by division, pull the plants apart and discard the woody interior growth. Watering is critical: never let the plants dry out completely, but remember that overwatering causes leaves to blacken and drop off.

Cinnamomum camphora
(Camphor Tree)
All zones except 2. Native to China. This is a slow-growing, stately, round-headed, evergreen tree which reaches a height of 15m (50ft) or more. It has a dark, heavy trunk and branches, and 10cm-long (4in), light green, shiny leaves; new spring foliage is bronze-red. The leaves give off a camphorous aroma when crushed. Clusters of tiny, yellow, fragrant flowers are borne in spring, followed by small dark fruits. This plant needs plenty of room: invasive roots make it a poor choice for garden beds, or near paths and walls. Propagate from seed.

Cistus
(Rockrose)
Evergreen shrubs. All zones but 6. These drought-resistant, fast-growing plants provide a colourful display of flowers in the spring and summer. Propagate from cuttings.

C. hybridus
(White Rockrose)
Grows to 1.5m (5ft) high and wide, with 5cm-long (2in), grey-green, rippled, fragrant leaves. The 4cm (1in) flowers, white with yellow centres, are borne through spring and summer.

C. purpureus
(Orchid Rockrose)
This cistus is the same size as *C. hybridus*, but it has a more compact shape. The green leaves have grey, whiskered undersides. The reddish-purple flowers, 8cm (3in) in diameter, have a red spot at the petal base.

Chrysanthemum frutescens (Marguerite Daisy)

Small, hibiscus-like, spotted flowers, rose to purple, provide a spectacular flower show in the autumn. It needs fast-draining, sandy soil and deep, infrequent watering once a month: reduced watering in late summer will produce more flowers.

Chrysanthemum
There are many species of chrysanthemums. The two listed below are those that will survive in the Arabian peninsula. Propagate from cuttings or by division.

C. frutescens
(Marguerite Daisy)
All zones. This fast-growing perennial bears white or yellow, daisy-like flowers almost all year round. It grows to 1m (3ft) high and wide and has deeply lobed leaves. It likes to be pruned regularly but lightly; it does not flower on older, woody growth.

C. morifolium
('Florists Mum')
All zones but 6. This species provides a wide range of the types of chrysanthemum flower seen in flower shops: pompons, daisy, cushion, spider and so on. It is doubtful whether you will be able to grow in your garden the profuse, showy chrysanthemums you buy in the shops. These are force-grown in regulated light

Citrus-Clytostoma

C. villosus
Similar to *C. purpureus*, but the whiskered leaves are green on both sides, and are more oval-shaped than *C. hybridus* or *C. purpureus*. The flowers are pinker.

Citrus
Evergreen landscape and fruit-producing trees and large shrubs. All zones but 6 and tender in areas of zones 2 and 4 where temperatures reach −5°C (23°F). Citrus make attractive, clear, dense, round-headed landscape trees. Normal varieties reach 6-7m (20-23ft), but dwarf varieties of 2-3m (7-10ft) are available. These make good patio, pool, or container trees or multi-trunk shrubs. The oval, pointed, dark green leaves vary in length from 7 to 15cm (3-6in), depending on the fruit type and variety. Small, creamy-white, fragrant flowers are produced, usually in the spring, followed by the fruit. Some varieties have thorns. Propagate by grafting onto rootstock.

All citrus must be planted in fast-draining sandy soil, preferably with at least 30% peat moss included as the organic material. They are shallow-rooted, and so a 5-7cm (2-3in) mulch of peat moss or bark should always be applied, reaching out past the drip line of the tree, to help keep the upper roots moist and cool. Citrus require watering more often than other trees – daily during the hottest months – but do not let the soil become saturated. Water deeply with a hose trickling near the trunk, once or twice a month. Fertilize with a high nitrogen fertilizer in February, early May, and late August.

Fruit production is greatest on the lower branches and so, where possible, trees should be pruned so that branching starts approximately 1m (3ft) above ground. This makes harvesting easier and prevents the heavily laden lower branches drooping to the ground, where contact with the moist soil may cause rotting.

The trunk and main branches are susceptible to sunburn, so they should be covered with burlap, paper, or a water-based paint during the hotter months.

Listed below are those fruit types that have been tried successfully in the Middle East, but check with your local nursery for the varieties that do well in your area:

Bears Lime
Calamondin Orange
Citrus aurantium (Sour Orange)
Eureka Lemon
Mandarin Orange (Tangerine)

Marsh Seedless Grapefruit
Navel Orange
Tangelo
Valencia Orange

Clerodendron inerme
(Wild Jasmine)

Clematis armandii
(Evergreen Clematis)
An evergreen clematis. Zones 1,3,5. Sensitive to salts. This is a far-reaching vine, difficult to establish, but fast-growing thereafter. The glossy, dark green leaves are divided into three 8-10cm-long (3-4in), drooping leaflets. Large, branched clusters of 7cm (3in), white, star-like flowers are borne in mid-spring. Needs regular pinching and pruning. Propagate from seed or cuttings.

Clerodendron inerme
(Wild Jasmine)
Arabic: *Yasmin Zefer*
A popular evergreen vine, shrub. All zones. Native to northern India. Salt-tolerant to 8,000 ppm. This is widely used either as a spreading shrub or as a vine cascading over walls. The dense, lush foliage consists of 8-10cm-long (3-4in), dark green, oval leaves. Small, white, five-petaled flowers are borne, somewhat sparsely, in early summer. It is easy to establish and needs little pruning. It may show chlorosis: if affected treat with chelated iron. Propagate from cuttings.

Clytostoma callistegioides
(Lavender Trumpet Vine)
Evergreen. Zones 1,3,5,7. This vine attaches itself to open structures with tendrils. It may burn in hot sun, but does well in shade. The 10cm-long (4in), oval, pointed leaves consist of two leaflets with rippled edges. 8cm-long (3in),

Cockscomb-Coriandrum

Ripening coconuts
(*Cocos nucifera*)

lavender, trumpet-shaped flowers are borne
from spring to autumn. Prune back heavily in
winter. Propagate from cuttings.

Cockscomb: see *Celosia*

Coconut Palm: see *Cocos*

Cocos
Tall, slim-trunked palms reaching 16m (53ft),
with long, arching, feathery fronds.

C. nucifera
(Coconut Palm)
Zones 1,5,7. This is the coconut-producing
palm of the tropics. It requires a warm and
humid environment. The coconut itself is a
seed, and it is propagated as follows: bury the
coconut on its side (husk and all) in a large pot
or container, filled with soil rich in organic
matter; the coconut should be two-thirds
covered in soil. Keep the soil moist, but not
saturated, and place the container in a warm,
lighted area, but not in direct sunlight. Within
10-12 weeks it should produce a root system
and a shoot coming out of the narrow end.
When the shoot appears, cut back the watering
somewhat, and move the plant into an area
where it will get full sun in winter, but only
morning sun in the summer.

C. plumosa (arecastrum romanzoffianum)
(Queen Palm)
Zones 1,(3),5,7. A fast-growing, graceful,
straight-trunked palm which will grow in zone
3 if kept in shade from late spring to early
autumn, or on the east or north side of a
building. The glossy, bright green leaves will
rip and tatter in the wind.

Conocarpus lancifolia
(Button Mangrove)
An evergreen tree or large shrub. Zones 1,3,5,7.
This is a fast-growing and attractive ornamental
tree reaching 6.5m (22ft). It is suitable for large
gardens or parks. The 15-20cm (6-8in) narrow,
lance-like leaves are dark green. Small, creamy-
white spring flowers are followed by red,
pepper-like fruit. It does best in soil rich in
organic material. Propagate from seed or cuttings.

Convolvulus mauritanicus
(Ground Morning Glory)
An evergreen ground cover. All zones. Native to
Africa. Reaches a height of 15-20cm (6-8in) and
a spread of 1m (3ft). The small, fuzzy, round-to-
oval leaves are grey-green; the lavender-blue
flowers, 3-4cm (1-1½in) in diameter, bloom in
summer. This is an informal ground cover that
needs heavy winter pruning; alternatively use in
a hanging basket.

Coral Gum: see *Eucalyptus*

Coral Tree: see *Erythrina*

Coral Vine: see *Antigonon*

Cordia sebestina
(Scarlet Cordia)
An evergreen small tree or large shrub. Zones
1,3,5,7. Native to the West Indies. This round-
headed tree with brown, ridged bark, needs
staking if trained as a standard tree. It is
attractive as a multi-trunk. The large oval to
heart-shaped leaves are rough-textured, with
clusters of bright red, 10cm (4in) flowers,
followed by berry-like fruit. It requires regular
pruning to maintain a balanced shape, and
tends to be messy, with leaves shedding all year.
Propagate from seed.

Coriandrum sativum
(Coriander)
All zones. This is an aromatic annual herb used
in Lebanese and Arabic cooking. It reaches 30-
40cm (12-14in) high and wide, with feathery,
fern-like foliage. The leaves are used in salads,
soups, and poultry dishes; the seeds are used,
crushed, in lamb recipes, stews and biscuits.

Cortaderia-Cynadon

The small, pinkish-white flowers are borne in flat clusters, 10cm (4in) in diameter. Propagate from seed.

Cortaderia selloana
(Pampas Grass)
A huge, ornamental grass. All zones. Native to Argentina. Salt-tolerant to at least 7,000 ppm. Forms a giant clump of fast-growing, saw-toothed grass leaves, with tall stalks of lovely, large, feathery, white or pink plumes in summer. This is a plant that needs space; it is not for small gardens. If it goes ratty and brown-looking, burn it to the ground; it will rapidly regrow. Propagate from seed.

Cotinus coggygria
(Smoke Tree)
Deciduous. All zones. Very drought-tolerant. This is a wide-spreading, urn-shaped tree or large shrub reaching 8m (27ft). The 5-8cm-long (2-3in), roundish leaves are blue-green in summer, turning yellow to orange-red in the autumn. As the tiny purple flowers fade in mid-summer, the stalks elongate and are covered with smoke-like, thin, lavender hairs. It requires a fast-draining soil and infrequent watering.

Council Tree: see *Ficus*

Crape Myrtle: see *Lagerstroemia*

Crown of Gold Tree: see *Cassia*

Cupressocyparis leylandii
(Leyland Cypress)
An evergreen tree. All zones. This is a fast-growing conifer reaching 15-20m (50-65ft) with a symmetrical, narrow, pyramidal shape. Flat, fan-like, grey-green foliage is carried on long, slender branches. It makes an attractive screening tree. Propagate from cuttings.

Cupressus
(Cypress)
Coniferous evergreen trees with tiny scale-like leaves or needles. Propagate from seed or cuttings.

C. glabra
(Arizona Cypress)
All zones. Drought-resistant, and salt-tolerant to 2,500 ppm. This fast-growing tree reaches 12m (40ft) high and 6m (20ft) wide. The foliage is light green to blueish-grey; the bark is smooth and red. A good screening tree.

C. sempervirens
(Italian Cypress)
All zones. This tall, slender, dark green conifer is widely used in Mediterranean formal gardens, and flanking driveways. Like many conifers it is susceptible to spider mites.

Cycas revoluta
(Sago Palm)
Zones 1,3,5,7. A decorative, palm-like plant. Stiff, fern-like, 60cm-long (24in) leaves grow out of the top of the trunk. This is a very slow-growing plant which reaches 3m (10ft) and produces offsets ('pups'). It makes an excellent container plant and is also suitable for tropical gardens, but it will not tolerate full afternoon sun. It should be grown on the east or north side of a building or wall, or with winter sun and summer shade. Propagate from seed or offsets.

Cynadon dactylon
(Bermuda Grass)
All zones. Salt-tolerant to at least 5,000 ppm. The most widely grown plant in the world. A fine-leafed grass of a slightly greyish-green colour, which spreads by runners and rhizomes. It can be very invasive, and very difficult to get rid of in areas where not desired, thus its nickname "devil grass". If it is properly fertilized with a high nitrogen fertilizer, and mowed regularly, it will make an attractive lawn. The 15-20cm (6-8in) seed stalks have 3-6 spikes emanating from the top. This is the most

A young *Cortaderia selloana* (Pampas Grass)

Cyperus-Cytisus

widely used grass for lawns in the Middle East. It will form a thick undergrowth or "thatch" if it is not regularly mowed short to 2-3cm (1in). Propagate from seed or stolons (dry roots).

Cyperus alternifolius
(Umbrella Plant)
Zones 1,3,5,7. This is a rush- or grass-like water plant, which tolerates shade, and is suitable as a house plant. The thin, radiating leaves (like the ribs of an umbrella) are carried at the top of 70-120cm (28-48in) stems. The flowers are borne in greenish-brown clusters. It can be grown in moist soil or water. This is a good container plant, but it is most effective in or near pools or stream beds. Propagate from seed or by division.

Cypress: see **Cupressus**

Cytisus, Genista, Spartium
(Brooms)
Evergreen or deciduous shrubs. Some species have insignificant leaves, and the plant's green or grey-green appearance is due mainly to the many stems. They are valued most for their sweet pea-like flowers, but generally do not do well in highly alkaline soils, or if subjected to highly saline water. Propagate from seed or cuttings.

C. canariensis
(Canary Island Broom)
Evergreen. All zones. This is a stiff shrub which reaches a height of 2m (6ft) and not quite as wide. The bright green leaves are divided into tiny leaflets. Yellow, fragrant flowers are borne in clusters at the ends of branches, during spring and summer.

C. praecox
(Moonlight Broom)
All zones but 6. A rounded, compact shrub to 1.8m (6ft) which may spread wider than high. It is covered with light yellow to creamy-white flowers in spring.

C. (Genista) racemosa
(Scottish Broom)
Evergreen. All zones. Similar to C. canariensis, but with larger leaflets, and longer, looser flower spikes.

C. (Spartium) junceum
(Spanish Broom)
All zones. A dense, erect, 2-3m (7-10ft) shrub with almost leafless stems. Bright yellow, fragrant flowers are borne in spring and summer, followed by fuzzy 10cm (4in) seed pods. This is a somewhat stark-looking shrub, which is suited to native desert gardens.

Dahlia-Datura

D

Dwarf *Dahlia*

Dahlia

Perennial tuber. All zones, but some varieties may need protection from the summer sun. Native to Mexico and Guatemala. Dahlias offer a spectacular variety of flower colours, types and sizes. Plant size varies from 2m (6½ft) shrubs down to 40cm (16in), compact bedding plants. The round to oval, 5-8cm-long (2-3in) leaves are dark green. Flowers range from button-sized pompons, to the single anemone type and giant decorative doubles. Dahlias are available in virtually all colours except blue. The dwarf varieties are planted from seed. If the leaves drop in the winter, cut the plant back to 10cm (4in) above the ground, and it will regrow in the spring. Tubers of the larger dahlias should be planted in the spring, 80-120cm (32-48in) apart. Dig a hole 30cm (12in) deep, then mix a planting soil with ⅓ organic material ⅓ sand and ¼ cup of complete fertilizer. Put 10cm (4in) of soil in the hole, then place the tuber horizontally in the soil mix. Cover with 10cm (4in) of soil, and water thoroughly. As the shoots grow, gradually fill in the hole. During the growing season, fertilize with superphosphate only.

On tall-growing varieties, thin out to the strongest 2 or 3 shoots. When these are leafed out, pinch off the terminal shoots to encourage bushiness. To produce larger flowers, pinch off all but the terminal buds on the side shoots.

Dahlias make excellent cut flowers. Pick them just before they are fully opened, then place the cut stems in 8cm (3in) of hot water. Leave them to stand overnight while the water cools, and then transfer them to a vase or arrangement.

Daisy, Trailing African: see *Osteospermum*

Daisy, Marguerite: see *Chrysanthemum*

Date Palm: see *Phoenix dactylifera*

Datura

(Angel's Trumpet)
Evergreen shrubs. Zones 1,3,5,7. These large-leafed, tubular-flowered plants bloom in late spring. The seeds and flowers are poisonous, but have been used in producing medicines. Datura require heavy pruning in early spring to avoid becoming rangy, and protection from the wind. Propagate from seed or cuttings.

Datura-Dill

Delonix regia (Royal Poinciana)

D. candida
Native to Peru. This fast-growing shrub reaches 3-4m (10-13ft) in height and 2-3m (7-10ft) in width. It has large (20-30cm/8-12in), dull green leaves. The 20cm (8in), white flowers, veined with green, are particularly fragrant at night.

D. inoxia
(Flora Plena)
Small shrub. Native to India. Reaches a height of 1m (3ft). The leaves are smaller and more oval-shaped than those of *D. candida*. 8-10cm (3-4in), white, trumpet-shaped flowers are borne at the end of branches in early summer, followed by 2-3cm (½-1in), globular, green fruit. This makes a good filler plant for gardens and small landscapes.

Day Lily: see *Hemerocallis*

Delaspermum: see **Ice Plant**

Delonix regia
(Royal Poinciana)
Deciduous tree. Native to Madagascar. All zones but 6. Tolerates salinity to 2,500 ppm. This very popular, large, round-headed tree reaches 13m (45ft) high. The bipinnate, 50-60cm-long (20-24in) leaves have dark green, 3cm-long (7in) leaflets; new foliage is a light emerald green. This is an excellent shade tree for

parks, roadways, and large gardens. The brilliant, 10cm (4in) in diameter, yellow to orange to red flowers have paddle-shaped petals which radiate outward from a red core. Flower clusters appear at the ends of branches from May to August. Blooms more profusely in coastal areas than inland. Propagate from seed.

Desert Gum: see *Eucalyptus*

Desert Willow: see *Chilopsis*

Dewdrop, Golden: see *Duranta*

Dianthus
Perennials, annuals. All zones, but need protection from afternoon summer sun. Over 300 species; here we describe the three most commonly planted. These make attractive garden plants, both for their flowers, which bloom from spring to autumn, and for their grass-like, narrow foliage. They are also excellent as cut flowers. Propagate annuals from seed, perennials from cuttings.

D. allwoodii
Perennial. These English hybrids (known as 'modern pinks') reach 10-60cm (4-24in) high, with dense tufts of blue-grey leaves. Single or double flowers are borne in a wide variety of colours.

D. barbatus
(Sweet William)
Annual biennial. The sturdy stems with 4-8cm (1½-3in) leaves reach a height of 20-70cm (8-28in). Large, dense clusters of small, white to rose-purple flowers are borne.

D. caryophyllus
(Carnation)
Perennial. These florist carnations have stems 1m (3ft) high or more with blueish-grey leaves. The stems tend to become woody at the base. A wide range of flower colours is available, including variegated. To produce larger flowers, pinch off all but the terminal bud on each stem. Needs staking.

Other varieties, called 'border carnations', are bushier, more compact, and more attractive as garden plants. Profuse, 5-7cm (2-3in) flowers are borne in white, salmon, rose or red. Some varieties are very fragrant. They make excellent border or container plants.

Dill: see *Anethum*

Dodonea-Dusty Miller

Dodonea viscosa
(Hopseed Bush)
Arabic: *Sheth*
Evergreen shrub. All zones. Drought-tolerant, salt-tolerant to 7,000 ppm. This is a very versatile, dense, deep green shrub reaching 4m (13ft) which can be pruned as a standard or multi-trunk tree. The narrow, 15cm-long (6in) leaves are oblong. Insignificant greenish flowers are followed by clusters of tan-brown, winged seed capsules in the autumn. It can be clipped as a formal hedge, or used as a screen or background plant. Needs well-drained soil. Propagate from seed.

Doxantha unguis-cati
(Cat's Claw Vine)
Semi-deciduous. All zones. This is a fast-growing vine with claw-like, forked tendrils, and leaves that are pairs of 5cm-long (2in), glossy green leaflets. 5cm-long (2in), tubular, yellow flowers are borne in early spring. To maintain the plant's bushiness, prune it throughout the year, and heavily after flowering. Propagate from cuttings.

Drosanthemum: see **Ice Plant**

Drumstick Tree: see *Moringa*

Duranta
Evergreen shrubs. Zones 1,3,5,6,7. The glossy, dark green leaves are carried in pairs or whorls. Blue flower clusters are borne in late spring and summer, followed by bunches of yellow berries. Both species need lots of water and regular pruning.

D. erecta
(Golden Dewdrop)
This fast-growing shrub reaches a height of 5m (17ft). Many stems can be pruned to make an attractive multi-trunk tree. The drooping branches sometimes have sharp spines. It has 3cm (1in), rounded leaves, and small, tubular, lavender-blue flowers.

D. stenostachya
(Brazilian Skyflower)
This is a smaller, more compact shrub that *D. erecta*, but with larger, tapering, pointed leaves, and slightly larger flowers. The branches are spineless.

Dusty Miller: see *Senecio*

Echeveria-Equisetum

E

Erythrina caffra
(Kaffirboom Coral
Tree)

Echeveria
Succulents. Zones 1,3,5,7. All varieties have
rosettes of fleshy green, grey-green or variegated
leaves. Red, pink, or yellow bell-shaped flowers
are borne on long, slender stems in spring. Use
as container plants or for desert gardens.
Propagate from seed or from offsets.

E. agavoides
The 15-20cm (6-8in) rosettes have bright
green, smooth, stiff, pointed leaves, sometimes
with reddish-brown tips and edges. Small red
and yellow flowers are carried on 40cm-long
(6in) stalks.

E. elegans
(Hen and Chicks)
Produces many offsets with 10cm (4in), tight,
greyish-white rosettes. The yellow-lined, pink
flowers are carried in 20cm (8in) clusters.

E. imbricata
(Hen and Chicks)
Grey-green, 10-15cm (4-6in), saucer-like
rosettes. Many offsets.

Echinocactus: see **Cactus**

Echium fastuosum
(Pride of Madeira)
Evergreen shrub. All zones. A round-headed

shrub reaching 2m (6ft). The narrow, grey-
green, fuzzy leaves are carried in round clusters
at the stem ends. 20-30cm-long (8-12in),
tapering spikes of small lavender-blue flowers
grow above the foliage in spring and early
summer. This is a colourful, contrasting shrub
which will provide bold accents in a garden.
Light pruning and pinching are needed to keep
it bushy. Propagate from seed.

Eleagnus pungens
(Silverberry)
Evergreen shrub. All zones. This is a large shrub
reaching a height of 4m (13ft), but it is denser
and more attractive if kept pruned to a smaller
size. The silvery-green, 7cm-long (3in) leaves
have wavy edges. The branches and foliage are
spotted with brown, rusty dots. The
insignificant flowers are followed by silvery-red
fruits. Useful for screens or as a background
plant.

Ensete: see **Musa**

Equisetum hyemale
(Horsetail Reed)
Perennial. All zones. This primitive, rush-like
reed, has 1-1.5m-high (3-5ft) hollow, bright
green stems that have black or brown rings at
each joint, and cone-like spikes at the end of
each stem. The main stem may have whorls of

Eriobotrya-Eucalyptus

small, slender, jointed stems that radiate from joints. This is an effective plant around natural pools, but it is invasive, and is best kept in containers. Propagate from seed or by division.

Eriobotrya japonica
(Loquat)
Evergreen tree. All zones. A round-headed tree reaching 8m (27ft). The large, heavily veined, saw-toothed leaves, 15-30cm (6-12in) long and 5-10cm (2-4in) wide, are deep green and glossy on top, rush-coloured and fuzzy on the underside. The new branches are also 'woolly'. Clusters of small white flowers are borne in the autumn, followed by 3-5cm-long (1-2in), yellowish-orange, sweet, fragrant fruits with large seeds. If growing for the fruit, thin the interior branches to allow sunlight and remove one-third to one-half of any new loquats to allow these remaining to increase in size. This is a good tree for small gardens, patios, or large containers. It likes heavy watering. Propagate from seed or cuttings.

Erythea
These decorative fan palms can provide an effective focal point in patios or small gardens.

E. armata
(Mexican Blue Palm)
Zones 1,5. This drought- and wind-resistant, slow-growing palm reaches 12m (40ft) with foliage spreading 2-2.5m (6½-8ft). The leaves are a unique, silvery-blue. The creamy-white flowers are borne on short stalks.

E. edulis
(Guadalupe Palm)
Zones 1,3,5,7. Similar to *E. armata*, but the leaves are light green and the flowers are inconspicuous. The trunk is ringed with scars where old fronds have dropped off.

Erythrina
(Coral Tree)
Deciduous, semi-deciduous. These are brilliant flowering trees with light orange to flame-red blooms, and noteworthy branching structures. The leaves are divided into 3 leaflets.

E. caffra
(Kaffirboom Coral Tree)
Zones 1,3,5 (when young, protect from summer sun in zone 3). Salt-tolerant to 2,000 ppm. Semi-deciduous. Native to Southern Africa. This is a stately, wide-spreading shade tree, which reaches 12m (40ft) high, 16m (53ft) wide. The 8cm-long (3in) pointed leaflets may drop briefly in January or February. Large clusters of vivid red-orange, tubular flowers appear while the tree is deciduous. This is a spectactular smooth-barked, multi-trunk or low-branched tree for large gardens or parks. The thorns disappear on older branches. Propagate by cuttings, including large branches placed in the soil or a large container.

E. coralloides
Zones 1,3,5,7. Native to Mexico. Deciduous. The ungainly growth habit reaches 10m (33ft) in height and width. The drooping branches which carry large leaves, 20-25cm-long (8-10in), need regular pruning to maintain an attractive, balanced appearance. Bright red, candle-like, spring blossoms are borne at the tips of the thorny branches.

E. humeana
(Natal Coral Tree)
Deciduous. Zones 1,3,5,7. Native to Southern Africa. Grows to 10m (33ft). Orange-red blossoms are borne in summer and autumn at branch ends, above the deep green, heart-shaped leaflets.

Espostoa: see Cactus

Eucalyptus
Arabic: *Keena-Kaphour*
Evergreen trees and shrubs. Native to Australia. Drought-tolerant. The varieties seen in the Middle East are those that serve as tall screens or windbreaks. The generally attractive, fragrant foliage is frequently subject to yellowing by chlorosis (treat with iron chelate). When buying eucalyptus, select those that are somewhat small for their container size. Rootbound plants may never grow much larger than the size they are when planted. The rather messy leaf drop happens all year round. Propagate from seed.

E. camaldulensis (rostrata)
(Red Gum)
All zones. Salt-tolerant to 9,000 ppm. This is a tall, generally uneven tree reaching 25-30cm (85-100ft). The smooth, whitish bark peels yearly. The green leaves are narrow, and sometimes scimitar-shaped. The flowers are insignificant. This is the hardiest, and the most widely planted eucalypt in the Midde East.

Eucalyptus camaldulensis
(Red Gum)

Eucalyptus-Evening Primrose

E. rudis
(Desert Gum)

All zones. This symmetrical, somewhat spreading tree, reaching 20m (67ft) high, 8m (27ft) wide, has attractive, greenish-blue foliage with semi-oval, 15cm (6in) pointed leaves, and rough, tannish bark on older specimens. The clusters of small white flowers are insignificant. Its distinctive colour and even, tapering shape make it one of the more pleasing eucalpyts.

E. sideroxylon
(Pink Ironbark)

All zones. This is a 7-20m (23-67ft) high tree of varying shape, with rough, dark bark, and a light blueish tinge to the narrow, pointed, 15cm (6in) leaves. The pendulous clusters of pink flowers are borne from autumn to spring, followed by goblet-shaped seed capsules.

E. torquata
(Coral Gum)

Zones 1,3,5,7. A small, slender tree reaching 6m (20ft) with long, narrow, light green leaves and rough, flakey bark. Notable clusters of coral red to yellow flowers are borne. This is a good, colourful tree for a small garden; it can be trained to an even, graceful shape.

Euonymus japonica
(Evergreen Euonymous)

All zones. This dense, upright shrub, reaching 3m (10ft) high and 1.8m (4ft) wide, can be pruned as a small standard or multi-trunk tree. The thick, glossy, deep green, 5cm-long (2in) leaves are oval. Some varieties have variegated leaves. It is subject to mildew in coastal areas; also watch out for scale, thrips, and mites. This is a good background or filler shrub. Propagate from cuttings.

Evening Primrose: see *Oenothera*

F

Faftan Calotrope: see *Calotropis*

Feijoa sellowiana
(Pineapple Guava)
Zones 1,3,5,7. Native to South America.
Evergreen large shrub or small tree. This many-
stemmed shrub, reaching a height of 7m (25ft),
is adaptable to pruning as a standard or multi-
trunk tree. The glossy, oval, dark green, 6cm-
long (2in) leaves have silvery-white undersides.
The interesting, 3cm (1in) spring flowers have a
tuft of dark red stamens, surrounded by white,
purple-tinged petals. The light green, pulpy
fruits may not appear in inland desert areas.
This is a good, dense shrub for screening.
Propagate from cuttings.

Fern, Asparagus: see *Asparagus*

Ferocactus: see *Cactus*

Festuca ovina glauca
(Blue Fescue)
All zones. This blueish-grey ornamental grass
grows in clumps 20-30cm (8-12in) high and
wide. Its interesting colour and texture make it a
good contrast plant, or ground cover when
planted close enough (15-20cm/6-8in). When
the plant begins to look shabby, cut it to within
5cm (2in) of the ground. Divide overgrown
plants; also propagate from seed.

Ficus
Ornamental figs. Worldwide, this genus
contains a great variety of evergreen or
deciduous trees, shrubs, vines and house plants.
All they have in common is that they bear some
form of fig. Propagate from cuttings.

F. altissima
(Council Tree)
Evergreen. Zones 1,5,7. This large, wide-
spreading, banyan-like tree reaches 12m (40ft)
high and 20m (67ft) wide. The bark is silver-
grey, and the smooth, leathery leaves reach
20cm (8in) in length, with prominent ivory to
reddish veins. Profuse clusters of yellow-
orange to red, berry-like figs are borne. This is
a bold, magnificent tree for parks or large
gardens. Propagate from cuttings.

F. benghalensis
(Banyan Tree)
Evergreen. Zones 1,3,5,7. Salt-tolerant to
4,500 ppm. A wide-spreading, dense tree
reaching 15m (50ft) high and 18m (60ft) wide.

Ficus benghalensis
(Banyan Tree)

It has smooth, grey bark and leathery,
elliptical, glossy, 20cm-long (8in) leaves. The
inconspicuous flowers are followed by stalkless
pairs of red, cherry-like figs. This is a splendid,
clean shade tree for parks or large gardens.

F. benjamina
(Weeping Chinese Banyan)
This is primarily an indoor tree, but it can be
grown in shade or morning sun in zones 1,3,5.
It is dense and shrubby with 10cm-long (4in),
oval, dark green, poplar-like leaves. It is
excellent as a container plant, or as an espalier.

F. microphylla
Evergreen tree. Zones 1,3,5. Round-headed,
reaching 10m (33ft); leaves similar to *F.
benghalensis*, but smaller and more oval. A good
tree for courtyards and patios.

F. nitida (retusa nitida)
(Indian Laurel)
Evergreen tree. Zones 1,3,4,5,7. Salt-tolerant
to 5,000 ppm. This is a dense, adaptable tree,
eventually growing to 13m (45ft), with
leathery, deep green, pointed oval, 10cm-long
(4in) leaves and smooth, tannish-grey bark.
They are widely used as street trees, and can
also be clipped to formal globe or cube shapes.
Also sometimes used as dense screens. They
bear grey-green, berry-like figs. Subject to
scale, and to thrips which cause the leaves to
curl; treat with Basudin or Malathion.

F. religiosa
(Peepul Tree)
Arabic: *Lesan al Asfour*
Semi-deciduous. Zones 1,3,5,7. Native to
India. This is a large tree with a somewhat
erratic growth habit reaching 20m (67ft)
height and spread. It needs regular pruning.
The 20cm-long (8in) leaves are oval. The new

Ficus-Fruit Trees

Ficus nitida (Indian Laurel)

growth is a pinkish-copper colour, and the bark is brown. This is a stately tree.

F. sycamoris
(Sycamore Fig)
Semi-deciduous. Zones 1,3,5,6,7. Native to Egypt and Syria. This is a large, round-headed tree with 15-25cm-long (6-10in), lobed, oval leaves, a lighter green than those of most *Ficus*. Clusters of small, berry-like figs are borne. Seen wild in wadis and escarpments.

Fig, Hottentot: see **Ice Plant**

Filmy Lily: see *Hymenocallis*

Flame Tree: see *Koelruteria*

Flax, New Zealand: see *Phormium*

Flora Plena: see *Datura*

Floss Silk Tree: see *Chorisia*

Fortnight Lily: see *Moraea*

Fountain Grass: see *Pennisetum*

Frangipani: see *Plumeria*

Frankincense: see *Boswellia*

Fraxinus
(Ash)
Deciduous, semi-evergreen trees. These are fast-growing shade trees that tolerate alkaline soil. Propagate from seed.

F. uhdei
(Shamel Ash)
Semi-evergreen. Zones 1,3,5,7. Native to Mexico. Pyramid-shaped when young, this tree spreads to a round-headed shape as it matures, reaching a height of 20m (67ft). The bipinnate leaves are divided into 5-9, saw-toothed, glossy green, 10cm-long (4in) leaflets. A good shade tree, best if protected from winds.

F. velutina 'Modesto'
(Modesto Ash)
Deciduous. All zones. Grows to 15m×9m (50×30ft). The glossy green leaflets are slightly smaller and a lighter green than *F. uhdei*. This is a fast-growing, hardy, symmetrical shade tree.

Fruit Trees, Deciduous
These showy, flowering, fruiting trees are limited to zones 2 and 4 with a few in zone 7, because of their requirement for cold winter temperatures. They include:
Almond
Apple
Apricot
Cherry
Nectarine
Peach
Plum

Some fruit trees require up to 70 days of below-freezing weather to set fruit successfully in the spring, others just a few days. They are characterized by showy displays of blossoms in spring, ranging from white to pink to red. Some, like the purple leaf plums, have distinctive, red to purple foliage. Some are non-fruiting. There are hundreds of varieties, with varying pollination requirements, so check with your local nurseries to see which are suitable.

Gamolepsis-Gazania

G

Gamolepsis crysanthemoides

Evergreen shrub. All zones. This fast-growing shrub reaches 1.8m (6ft) high and wide. The lacy, bright green foliage has deeply lobed, 8cm-long (3in) leaves. 4cm-wide (1½in), bright yellow, daisy-like flowers are produced almost continuously. It requires regular pruning and pinching to keep it evenly shaped. Propagate from seed or cuttings.

Gardenia jasminoides

(Gardenia)
Zones 1,3,5,7, but must be sheltered from hot afternoon summer sun. It should be grown on the east or north side of a building or wall. This is an excellent container plant, and can be grown indoors if it gets plenty of light. The bright green, glossy leaves are oval and the pure white, double flowers are fragrant.

Gardenias must have well-drained soil, with plenty of peat moss or ground bark (60-70%) in the soil mix. They should be planted slightly higher than the surrounding soil, which should be kept moist. They will not tolerate salty water. Feed with acid plant food or fish emulsion. They also need regular feeding with iron chelate to avoid chlorosis. Their attractive appearance is helped by regular spraying with water, except when in bloom. The two best known varieties are:

G.j. 'Mystery'

Grows to 2m (6½ft) high and wide. 10-12cm (4-5in) double flowers are borne in late spring and may bloom until November. The dark green, oval leaves are 8-10cm (3in) long.

G.j. 'Veitchii'

More compact and denser than 'Mystery', with smaller leaves and flowers, but a greater abundance of blooms on each stem.

Garlic

This popular, aromatic bulb is used for seasoning. For planting, try to buy mother bulbs (sets), available through nurseries; these are slightly different from those you buy in food stores. In zones 2 and 4, they should be planted in early spring, but in the other areas they can be planted all year round. Break the bulbs up into individual cloves, and plant base downward, 3-5cm (2in) deep in the soil, 5-10cm (2-4in) apart. Harvest 4-6 months later when the grassy tops start falling over. Air dry for 2-3 weeks, remove tops and roots, and store in a dry, cool place.

Gazania splendens

Gazania

Perennial. All zones but 6. Native to Southern Africa. These small, clumping or trailing plants give a bright, colourful display of flowers, 7-10cm (3-4in) in diameter, for most of the year. They make excellent, reliable ground cover, and are also useful in small borders, or as drifts of flowers in a free form garden. They get rangy and ugly if watered too often. Propagate from seed, cuttings or by division.

G. splendens

This gazania forms a clump of deeply lobed, 20-30cm-long (8-12in) leaves, dark green with grey-green undersides. Varieties are available in a myriad of flower colours, white, yellow, orange, pink, and red, some with interesting variegations.

G. uniflora

This is a trailing gazania, with silver-grey narrow leaves, and yellow, orange, white, or bronze flowers. It spreads by long, trailing stems. It makes an excellent ground cover, but is also useful in hanging baskets.

Geijera-Gum

Gomphrena globosa
(Globe Amaranth)

Geijera parvifolia
(Australian Willow)
Evergreen tree. All zones. Grows to 9m×6m (28×20ft). The small, drooping branches, with 10-15cm-long (4-6in) narrow leaves, provide a willowy, graceful appearance. Very little pruning is required. This is a good tree for a courtyard focal point, or planted in groups to create a grove effect. Propagate from seed.

Gelsemium sempervirens
(Carolina Jasmine)
Evergreen vine. All zones. The open network of long, streamer-like branches bear pairs of 8cm-long (3in), oval, shiny, dark green leaves. The small, 3cm-long (1in), tubular yellow flowers bloom in early spring, giving off a sweet fragrance. All parts of the plant are poisonous. Propagate from cuttings.

Genista: see Cytisus

Geranium: see Pelargonium

Germander: see Teucrium

Giant Reed: see Arundo

Gleditsia triacanthus inermis
(Honey Locust)
Deciduous tree. Zones 2,3,4,7. This is a fast-growing, spreading, thornless tree reaching 12-20m (40-67ft). It is generally deciduous from early winter to mid-spring. The bipinnate leaves have numerous 2-4cm (1in) leaflets. The insignificant flowers are followed by a few, 30-45cm-long (12-18in), hanging seed pods in summer. Needs staking and regular pruning when young. This makes a good lawn tree, but it has invasive roots, so keep it away from walls and paving. It does best in cold winters and hot summers. Propagate from seed.

Globe Amaranth: see Gomphrena

Goat's Foot Creeper: see Ipomoea

Golden Dewdrop: see Duranta

Goldenrain Tree: see Koelruteria

Gomphrena globosa
(Globe Amaranth)
Annual. All zones. This annual grows to a height of 30-80cm (12-32in) and has stiff branches and narrow, oval, fuzzy leaves, 5-10cm (2-4in) long. Stalks of small, globular, pink, purple or white flowers are borne in summer and autumn. Propagate from seed.

Grape
Deciduous vine. All zones. This is a very fast grower, which, once established, can produce enough new growth each year to roof an arbor, or arch over a walkway. The large, 10-15cm, tooth-edged leaves have a somewhat triangular shape. Clusters of small, whitish spring flowers are followed by pendulous fruit clumps. Careful, annual, heavy pruning is required for good fruit production. On most varieties initial pruning is needed to establish a strong single trunk as the base of the plant. Nitrogen and iron chelate are the only fertilizers needed.

Proven varieties are shown below:
White:	Thompson (seedless)
	Berlette (with seeds)
Red:	Flame (seedless)
	Ruby Red (with seeds or seedless)
Black:	Robair (with seeds)

Ground Morning Glory: see Convolvulus

Guadalupe Palm: see Erythea

Guava, Pineapple: see Feijoa

Gum: see Eucalyptus

Heavenly Bamboo-Hibiscus

H

Heavenly Bamboo: see *Nandina*

Hedera canariensis
(Algerian Ivy)
Evergreen vine, ground cover. All zones but 6.
The shallow-lobed, 12-20cm (5-8in), shiny,
dark green leaves are widely spaced on the dark
stems. It climbs rapidly by 'aerial rootlets' –
small roots emanating from the leaf nodes, that
can attach themselves to a vertical surface, like a
wall, by means of a glue-like substance, or twine
around the links of a chain link fence. This is a
wide-spreading ground cover with branches
that will send down roots into the soil. It is an
excellent, deep-rooted plant for stablizing soil
on a steep bank. The inconspicuous clusters of
greenish flowers are followed by black berries.
Feed with high Nitrogen fertilizer in spring and
late summer. Propagate from cuttings.

Helianthus annuus
(Sunflower)
Annual. All zones. This is a rough, ungainly
plant reaching 3m (10ft), with deep green,
heart-shaped, 15-20cm (5-8in) leaves. Its well-
known flowers consist of yellow, petal-like rays
surrounding heads of tiny disk flowers of yellow,
reddish-mahogany, or brown. The flowers are
anything from 15cm(6in) to a giant 25cm (10in)
across. Propagate from seed.

Helichrysum bracteatum
(Strawflower)
This is a fast-growing annual, reaching a height
and width of 60-80cm (24-32in), with
'everlasting' flowers; this means they can be
dried, and retain their shape and colour. Many
pompon-like flowers, 7cm (3in) in diameter, are
borne on each plant, in white, pink, red, yellow,
and orange; they also make good cut flowers.
Plant seed in spring or early summer. To dry
flowers, cut with 10-15cm (4-6in) of stem, then
hang upside down in a dark, dry room or closet
for 2-3 weeks.

Hemerocallis
(Day Lily)
Perennial with tuberous roots. All zones. There
are many varieties, some evergreen, some
deciduous. All plants have clumps of narrow,
upright, sword-like leaves, ranging from 30cm
(12in) dwarf grass-like varieties, up to 1.6m
(64in). The lily-like flowers bloom in spring and
summer in a large range of colours: white,
yellow, orange, rust, red, violet, and more, on
leafless stems that project above the foliage.

They make good cut flowers, lasting up to a
week, if cut just as the buds are opening. Flower
colours are brightest if they are shaded from
summer afternoon sun. These make good
container or border plants, and are effective if
grown amongst contrasting ground cover.
Propagate from seed or by division.

Hen and Chicks: see *Echeveria*

Herbs see pp. 19-20, and individual entries
elsewhere in the plant encyclopedia.

Hibiscus rosa-sinensis
(Chinese Hibiscus)
Evergreen shrub. Zones 1,3,5, may need frost
protection in 7. Native to China. Signs of stress,
and flowering is reduced, at salinity levels above
1,000 ppm. The even, rounded growth habit
reaches 4m (13ft). This is one of the showiest,
most colourful shrubs grown in the Middle East.
The deep green, oval leaves are 6-10cm (2½-
4in) long, depending on the variety. The large
single or double flowers are borne in a variety of
colours: red, yellow, pink, white, orange, coral.
In mild weather hibiscus may bloom
throughout the year; normally they bloom in
spring and autumn.
   Hibiscus need shady, fast-draining soil, and
like plenty of water, particularly during the
flowering season. They should be fed once a
month from spring to autumn with a complete
fertilizer. To keep plants dense and bushy, cut

Hibiscus rosa-sinensis
(Chinese Hibiscus)

Hollyhock-Hymenocallis

all stems back to about one quarter of their length in early spring; in addition pinching out the tips of stems in spring and summer will increase flower production. Hibiscus are hosts to aphids, scale and mites, and should be inspected regularly. They make good screening plants, as well as espaliers, or free-standing, multi-trunk trees. They can also be grown in large containers. Propagate from cuttings.

Some of the more colourful varieties are:
'Agnes Gault': large, pink, single flowers.
'Brilliant' (San Diego Red): a profusion of bright red single blooms.
'California Gold': double flowers with golden-yellow petals, reddish-orange throat.
'Kona': a vigorous, upright shrub. Ruffled pink, double flowers.
'Tangerine': large, bright orange blooms.
'White Wings': single, white, narrow-petaled flowers with red throat.

Hollyhock: see *Althea*

Honey Locust: see *Gleditsia*

Honeysuckle, Cape: see *Tecomaria*

Honeysuckle, Hall's: see *Lonicera*

Hopseed Bush: see *Dodonea*

Horsetail Reed: see *Equisetum*

Hymenocallis littoralis
(Filmy Lily)
Perennial. Zones 1,5,7. A tropical plant reaching a height of 90cm (36in) and a spread of 70cm (28in), with long, strap-like, arching leaves, and flower stalks carrying white, spider-like flowers with long, leggy petals. This is a good border or container plant. Propagate by division.

Iberis-Ice Plant

I

Iberis sempervirens
(Candytuft)
Perennial. All zones but 6. Ground cover or
small shrub. This shrub forms a clump, 15-30cm
(6-12in) high and 40-70cm (16-28in) wide. It
has small, narrow, dark green leaves and a
profusion of small white flowers borne in spring
and sporadically throughout the year. It is
similar to white alyssum, but is a perennial.
Propagate from seed.

Ice Plant
Succulent, perennial ground covers that flower
in spring and sometimes erratically throughout
the year. Drought- and salt-tolerant. All ice
plants need full sun and will die back if
overwatered. Feed with complete fertilizer in
spring and autumn. Easily propagated from
cuttings.

Carpobratus edulis
(Hottentot Fig)
All zones. Heavy-leafed and wide-spreading,
this ice plant reaches 25cm (10in) high and 1m
(3ft) wide, with sometimes noticeably open
stems. The pink and pale yellow flowers are
followed by sour but edible fruit. This is a
suitable plant for shallow banks or beaches.

Delaspermum alba
(White Ice Plant)
Zones 1,3,5,6,7. The small dark green leaves,
and the low, even spreading habit (12cm/5in
high and 60cm/24in wide) make this a good
lawn substitute; it roots from stems as it
spreads. The small white flowers are borne
very sparsely. This plant provides good erosion
control on steep banks.

Drosanthemum hispidum
(Rosea Ice Plant)
Zones 1,3,5,7. This ice plant reaches 12cm
(5in) in height and 45cm (18in) in spread. The
small, sometimes spotted leaves are light
green, and the brilliant, profuse flowers are
lavender-rose. The trailing stems root into the
soil, making this a good ground cover for steep
banks.

Lampranthus aurantiacus
(Orange Ice Plant)
Zones 1,3,5,7. The medium-sized leaves are
borne in a clumping to spreading growth habit
15cm (6in) high with a spread of 45cm (18in).
The brilliant, almost iridescent, orange flowers
form a colourful carpet.

(above) *Drosanthemum
hispidum* (Rosea Ice
Plant), (left)
Lampranthus aurantiacus
(Orange Ice Plant)

Ice Plant-Ivy

Malephora crocea

Lampranthus spectabilis
Zones 1,3,5,7. This is a similar plant to *L. aurantiacus*, but its foliage has a slight greyish tint, and the spectacular flowers are red, purple, pink or rose pink.

Malephora crocea
Zones 1,3,5,6,7. This trailing ground cover, which reaches a height of 15cm (6in) and a spread of 45cm (18in), has reddish-orange flowers, but less profuse than those of *Lampranthus aurantiacus*. It provides good erosion control on moderate slopes.

Indian Almond: see *Terminalia*

Inge dulce: see *Pithecolobium*

Ipomoea biloba (pes-caprae)
(Goat's Foot Creeper)
All zones. Evergreen vine. Salt-tolerant to 5,000ppm. The bright green, glossy leaves are divided into two segments which are joined by a major vein. The 8-12cm, trumpet-shaped, pink to mauve flowers are borne in spring. This is a good vigorous plant for walls or ground cover. Propagate from cuttings.

Ipomoea palmata
(Railway Creeper)
Zones 1,3,5,7. This is an evergreen vine, with deeply cut, seven-lobed leaves and pinkish-lavender, short-lived, trumpet flowers in spring. It tolerates both sun and shade.

Ivy, Algerian: see *Hedera*

Jacaranda-Jujube

J

Jacaranda acutifolia
(Jacaranda)
Deciduous to semi-deciduous tree. All zones but 6. Native to Brazil. This is an open-structured tree, reaching 12m×8m (40ft×27ft). The dark green, fern-like, bipinnate foliage is usually shed in February. New foliage may appear at once, or not until June. Clusters of striking, 5cm (2in), lavender-blue flowers are borne in May or June, followed by round, flat seed capusules. A stately standard tree, but also attractive as a multi-trunk or a low-branched specimen. Propagate from seed or cuttings.

Jasmine: see *Jasminum*

Jasmine, Carolina: see *Gelsemium*

Jasmine, Night-blooming: see *Cestrum*

Jasmine, Red: see *Quisqualis*

Jasmine, Wild: see *Clerodendron*

Jasminum
(Jasmine)
Evergreen to deciduous vines and shrubs. These plants are noted for their sweet fragrance, although some species are unscented. All need some pruning and pinching to achieve a desirable shape. Propagate from cuttings.

J. mesneyi
(Primrose Jasmine)
Evergreen shrub-vine. All zones but 6. The long, arching branches can be pruned to make a fountain-like shrub or can be trained onto a wall or a trellis as a vine. The dark green leaves have 3 small, lance-shaped leaflets, and the plant stems are square. The bright yellow, 5cm-long (2in), semi-double flowers bloom for 10-12 months of the year. Looks best if trained against the top of a wall or trellis, with the lateral growth allowed to cascade downward.

J. officinale
(White Jasmine)
Zones 1,3,5,7. Evergreen in most areas. The most commonly grown jasmine in the Middle East, *officinale* has long twining stems, bearing dark green leaves with 5-7, small, narrow leaflets. Loose clusters of 2-3cm (1in) white, star-like, fragrant flowers are borne in spring and summer. Difficult to establish, but fast-growing thereafter.

Jasminum mesneyi
(Primrose Jasmine)

J. polyanthum
(Pink Jasmine)
Evergreen vine. All zones. This is a fast-growing vine with finely divided leaflets; it is perhaps the most fragrant jasmine. The dense clusters of flowers, white inside, rose-pink outside, bloom from early spring throughout the summer. Also used as a ground cover.

J. sambac
(Arabian Jasmine)
Small evergreen shrub. Zones 1,3,5 (requires summer shade in zone 3). The dark green, smooth, oval to elliptical leaflets are carried in pairs. Clusters of white, star-like, very fragrant single or double flowers are scattered over the dense shrub in early summer. This is a delightful bush to add colour accents in gardens or on patios; it is one of the most popular shrubs grown in the region.

Jerusalem Thorn: see *Parkinsonia*

Joseph's Coat: see *Amaranthus*

Jujube: see *Zizyphus*

Kochia-Koelruteria

K

Kochia scoparia
(Summer Cypress)
Annual. All zones. This is an unusual plant with distinctive, emerald green, feathery foliage, and a rounded, cylindrical shape reaching a height of 90cm (36in). It makes an interesting low hedge or border. The flowers are insignificant. Propagate from seed.

Koelruteria
Deciduous trees. All zones but 6. Large, loose clusters of yellow flowers are born in summer. The colourful seed capsules resemble tiny Japanese lanterns.

K. bipinnata henryi
(Chinese Flame Tree)
This is a narrow, tapering tree when young, which spreads as it matures. Moderate growth to 12m (40ft). The 30-60cm-long (12-24in) leaves are divided into numerous oval leaflets and the flowers are showy and yellow to yellow-orange. Large clusters of orange to red, 5cm-long (2in) seed capsules are borne in late summer and autumn. It needs a well-drained soil, and staking and pruning to develop a pleasing shape. This is a good courtyard or lawn tree. Propagate from seed or cuttings.

K. paniculata
(Goldenrain Tree)
This is a more open-branched and wide-spreading tree than K. bipinnata. The 40cm (16in) leaves have many toothed or lobed 5cm-long (2in) leaflets. The seed capsules are brown. It is more vigorous, and drought- and wind-tolerant than K. bipinnata.

Lagerstroemia-Lavandula

L

Lagerstroemia indica
(Crape Myrtle)
Semi-deciduous. All zones, particularly zones
2,3 and 4, but mildew can be a serious problem
where humidity is high. Native to China. This is
a slow-growing small tree or large shrub
reaching 8m (27ft). It makes a very attractive
multi-trunk or low-branched tree. The smooth,
tannish-brown bark flakes off to reveal pink
inner bark. Young foliage is bronzy-red; older
leaves are oval, 3-5cm-long (1-2in), and a deep
glossy green. It puts on a spectactular flower
show in hot, dry areas, with clusters of 4cm (2in)
flowers at branch ends, in colours ranging from
bright red to lavender, rose, pink, and white. It
blooms in summer and autumn. It does not like
alkaline soil or saline water, so heavy leaching
may occasionally be necessary. It is also
sometimes chlorotic, but may be treated with
iron chelate or iron sulphate. This makes an
excellent small tree for patios and small gardens.
Propagate from cuttings.

Lampranthus: see **Ice Plant**

Lantana
Evergreen vining shrubs and ground covers. All
zones but 6. Native to China. Salt-tolerant to
3,000 ppm. These are very popular in the
Middle East. They are notable for their versatile
growth habits and almost year-round flowering
season. Compact varieties are available, and are
very popular. Propagate from cuttings.

L. camara
Whilst used primarily as a shrub, *L. camara* can
be trained vine-like against a wall. It will reach
3m (10ft) in height, but a denser and more
pleasing shape is obtained if it is pruned to 2m
(6½ft) or smaller. The 5-10cm-long (2-4in),
oval leaves are dark green and rough-textured.
Small, hemispherical flowers are borne in a
myriad of colours ranging from bright yellow to
orange, pink, red, and a combination of
colours. The green to blueish berries, borne in
the autumn, are poisonous. This is a very
versatile plant for natural screens, clipped
hedges, or ornamental colour.

L. montividensis (sellowiana)
(Trailing Lantana)
This vigorous, wide-spreading ground cover
can appear to be a sea of lavender. Profuse
clusters of tiny flowers cover each plant all
year, providing dramatic winter colour. The
small, saw-toothed leaves are dark green. It

Lantana camara

should be fertilized no more than twice a year
with a complete fertilizer. It likes a lot of water.

Lavandula
(Lavender)
Evergreen shrubs. All zones. Native to the
Mediterranean. These shrubs are noted for their
greyish to grey-green foliage, and for their
fragrance which is used in perfumes and sachets.
Plants should be kept dense and compact by
pruning after the blooms fade. Watering and
fertilizing should be infrequent. To make your
own fragrant sachets, strip the flower clusters
from the plant stems just as the colour shows;
then dry them in a cool, dark place.

L. spica/L. officinalis
(English Lavender)
This is the celebrated lavender used for
perfumes and sachets. It is a rounded shrub
reaching 1m (3ft) high, with narrow, grey 5cm-
long (2in) leaves. 1cm (½in) spikes of lavender
flowers are borne on 40-60cm (16-24in) stalks
in summer.

Lavandula-Loquat

Lantana montividensis
(Trailing Lantana)

L. stoechas
(Spanish Lavender)
This is a stocky, 80cm-high (32in) plant with
very small, narrow grey leaves. Dark purple,
tiny flowers are borne in dense short spikes,
topped with a tuft of purple bracts in spring
and summer.

Lavender: see **Lavandula**

Lavender Cotton: see **Santolina**

Lavender Trumpet Vine: see **Clytostoma
callistegioides**

Lemaireocereus: see **Cactus**

Lemon: see **Citrus**

Leucophyllum frutescens
(Texas Sage)
Evergreen shrub. All zones. Drought- and salt-
tolerant. This is a slow-growing shrub reaching
2m (6½ft) high and 1.5m (5ft) wide. The
silvery-grey foliage has a loosely branched
habit. Orchid-pink, bell-like blooms are borne
in late spring and summer. Propagate from
cuttings.

Leyland Cypress: see **Cupressocyparis**

Lily, Day: see **Hemerocallis**

Lily, Fortnight: see **Moraea**

Lily of the Nile: see **Agapanthus**

Lime: see **Citrus**

Limonium perezii
(Statice, Sea Lavender)
Perennial. Zones 1,3,5,7. The large, leathery
leaves reach 30cm (12in) in length (including
stalks). Profuse, tiny, purple flowers with white
centres are borne along many-branched, leafless
stems to 90cm (36in) in spring and summer.
This makes a good border plant providing
bright colour accents; it can also provide
interesting dried flowers or long-lasting cut
flowers. Propagate from seed.

Lippia: see **Phyla nodiflora**

Lobularia maritima
(Sweet Alyssum)
Annual. All zones. This is a colourful,
dependable bedding plant or ground cover. It
reaches 20-30cm (8-12in) high and 30-50cm
(12-20in) wide and has small, narrow, lance-like
leaves, and profuse, tiny, four-petaled flowers
that produce a show of solid colour, ranging
from white to pink, lavender-pink, and purple.
As the blooms fade and the plant becomes leggy,
cut it back halfway and another crop of flowers
will appear. It reseeds itself.

Locust, Black: see **Robinia**

Locust, Honey: see **Gleditsia**

Lombardy Poplar: see **Populus**

Lonicera japonica 'Haliana'
(Hall's Honeysuckle)
Evergreen vine. All zones. This is a wide-
ranging vine or ground cover, with deep green,
oval, 5-7cm-long (2-3in) leaves. 3-4cm-long (1-
1½in) fragrant, tubular white flowers with a
purple tinge are borne in spring and summer. It
needs heavy pruning once a year to prevent it
becoming woody. Propagate from cuttings.

Loquat: see **Eriobotrya**

Madagascar Periwinkle-Melaleuca

M

Madagascar Periwinkle: see *Catharanthus*

Majorana hortensis
(Sweet Marjoram)
This is a perennial herb but treated as an annual in cold areas. All zones. It forms a clump reaching a height of 60cm (24in), with tiny, oval, grey-green leaves; spikes of white flowers are carried in loose clusters at the top of the plant. It requires moist soil. The leaves (either fresh or dried) are popular for seasoning meats, stews, casseroles, salads and vinegar. Propagate from seed or cuttings, or by division.

Malephora: see **Ice Plant**

Malvaviscus arboreus
Evergreen shrub. Zones 1,3,5,7. Native to Mexico. This is a densely branched, upright shrub with an awkward growth habit; it needs regular pruning to keep a balanced shape. The dark green, oval, 10cm-long (4in) leaves have serrated edges. The rich red flowers have overlapping petals like an unopened hibiscus flower. It likes full sun but will grow in partial shade. It is susceptible to aphids and mites. Propagate from cuttings.

Manila Tamarind: see *Pithecolobium*

Maniltoa gemnipara
Semi-deciduous tree. Zones 1,3,5,6,7. Native to New Guinea. This open-foliaged, somewhat awkward tree reaches a height of 12m (40ft). The large, arching leaves have many small, blunt-edged leaflets. Clusters of creamy-white spring flowers are followed by tannish-brown, bean-like seed pods. Decorative if pruned regularly and well sheltered. Propagate from seed.

Marguerite Daisy: see *Chrysanthemum*

Marigold: see *Tagetes*

Marigold, Pot: see *Calendula*

Marjoram, Sweet: see *Majorana*

Mediterranean Fan Palm: see *Chamaerops*

Medicine Plant: see *Aloe*

Melaleuca
Evergreen trees and shrubs. Zones 1,3,5,7. The small, narrow, tapering leaves are similar to

Malvaviscus arboreus

those of callistemon; the flowers, with prominent stamens, are also similar. Melaleuca will survive poor soils and erratic watering. Propagate from seed.

M. nesophylla
(Pink Melaleuca)
This forms a large shrub or small tree, with ungainly, fast growth reaching 6-7m (20-23ft). Unpruned, the branches will grow gnarled, crooked, and may droop back to ground level. If pruned and shaped, however, this makes an attractive multi-trunk tree or shrub, with thick, spongy, tannish bark and small, grey-green, roundish leaves. It flowers most of the year with 3cm (1in), round, mauve brushes, turning to white. The blooms are scattered all over the tree. This is a good tree to plant near the beach, since it is resistant to the ocean's salt spray.

M. quinquenervia (leucadendron)
(Cajeput Tree)
The upright, open growth reaches a height of 7-12m (23-40ft). The rough, thick, spongy bark, tan to white, peels off in sheets. The light green, narrow, oval, 5-10cm (2-4in) leaves are turned reddish purple by frost. Yellowish white, 5-8cm (2-3in), brush-like flower spikes are borne in summer and autumn. This is a

Melia-Moraea

Melia azederach (China Berry)

8cm-long (3in), oval, saw-toothed leaves have a strong scent. Spikes of small purple flowers are borne in spring. Used to flavour mint tea.

M. rotundifolia
(Apple Mint)
This upright plant reaches a height of 80cm (32in). The grey-green, rounded, 5-10cm-long (2-4in) leaves are slightly hairy. Small spikes of purplish-white flowers are borne in spring. It is used in mint jellies and jams.

M. spicata
(Spearmint)
This plant reaches a height of 60cm (24in). It forms a mound of dark green, 5cm-long (2in), oval leaves, and spikes of purple flowers in spring. The leaves can be used (fresh or dried) in lamb dishes, cold drinks, or mint jelly.

Mesquite: see *Prosopis*

Mexican Blue Palm: see *Erythea*

Mexican Fan Palm: see *Washingtonia*

Mimosa: see *Albizzia*

Mint: see *Mentha*

Modesto Ash: see *Fraxinus*

Moraea
(Fortnight Lily)
All zones, but needs protection from the summer sun. Native to Southern Africa. The foliage consists of narrow, upright, sword-like leaves. The short-lasting, small, iris-like flowers are borne on branched stalks during 9-10 months of the year. The blooms usually appear at two-week intervals. Water frequently during flowering. Propagate from seed or by division.

M. bicolor
The clumps of sword-like leaves reach 60cm (24in) in height and width. The 5cm (2in) flowers are light yellow with maroon markings. This is a valuable garden plant for providing contrasting leaf shape. When the blooms fade, cut the stalks to the ground.

M. iridiodes
Forms clumps that are 80cm (32in) high and wide. The 8cm (3in) flowers, white with an orange and brown cast and purple markings, are borne on 1m (3ft) stalks. When the blooms

dramatic multi-trunk tree to provide highlights in a garden or create a forest effect.

Melia azederach
(China Berry)
Deciduous tree. All zones. Salt-tolerant to 6,000 ppm. This is a dense, round-headed shade tree reaching 12m (40ft). The 35-40cm-long (14-16in) leaves have narrow oval or scythe-shaped leaflets with saw-toothed edges. Loose clusters of small, white, honey-scented flowers are borne in summer, followed by white to yellow, berry-like fruits which are poisonous (although they are sometimes used for medicinal purposes). This makes an excellent, compact shade tree for courtyards, lawns, and large gardens. Propagate from seed.

Mentha
(Mint)
Perennial herbs and ground covers. All zones. These plants spread by underground stems (rhizomes). They do best in partial shade or morning sun. Propagate from seed or rhizomes.

M. piperita
(Peppermint)
This is a rounded plant reaching 1m (3ft). The

fade, cut the stalks close to the ground but leaving one or two nodes uncut.

Moringa oliefera
(Drumstick Tree)
Evergreen tree. Zones 1,3,5,7. Native to India. This is an erect-growing, open-structured tree reaching 7m (23ft). It has dark, corky bark and somewhat brittle branches. The bipinnate leaves are up to 45cm (18in) long, with numerous, 6-8cm-long (2½-3½in) leaflets. Large, loose clusters of creamy-white flowers that are sweetly scented are borne in spring. The bean-like, dark seed pods give the tree its name. It requires careful pruning to avoid the formation of tight crotches between branches. This is a good tree for light shade in courtyards and patios. Propagate from seed or cuttings.

Morus alba
(Fruitless Mulberry or Silkworm Mulberry)
Deciduous tree. All zones. This is a fast-growing, wide-spreading shade tree reaching 15m (50ft). It is tolerant of heat and alkaline soil. The variable-shaped leaves, sometimes lobed, heart-shaped or oval, are 8-15cm (3-6in). The trunk requires strong staking to accommodate the wide crown. Drooping branches should be pruned regularly. This is a good shade tree for lawns or large gardens. Propagate from cuttings.

Mother-in-Law's Tongue: see *Sanseveria*

Mother's Tongue: see *Albizzia*

Mulberry, Fruitless: see *Morus*

Musa (Ensete)
(Banana)
Tree-like tropical perennials. Zones 1,3, if protected from summer sun, and prominently in the Jordan river valley. Sensitive to salty water, and killed by frost. These plants have thick stems and huge, broad leaves that are easily ripped by wind. They must be grown in a sheltered location. They grow in clumps and spread by underground roots. They need soil rich in organic material and lots of water. Propagate from seed or by division.

M. cavendishii, M. nana
This plant may reach 3m (10ft), with leaves of 60-90cm (24-36in) × 30cm (12in). The new leaves are red, turning to a blotched, blueish green. 12cm-long (5in) yellow fruit, which are seedless and edible are produced in the spring and the autumn. This is the commercial banana.

M. paradisiaca semnifera
This banana reaches a height of 6m (20ft) with 2.5m-long (7ft) leaves. The occasional, drooping flower stalks, which bear small, yellow flowers with powdery, purple bracts, are followed by small, greenish-yellow, inedible fruit. This is a useful plant for a tropical effect.

Nandina-Night-blooming Jasmine

N

(above and right)
Nerium oleander
(Oleander)

Nandina domestica

(Heavenly Bamboo)
Evergreen shrub. All zones, but needs protection from summer sun. This is an upright plant, similar to bamboo, reaching a height of 2m (6½ft). The finely divided leaves have 3-5cm-long (1-2in), oval, pointed leaflets. The new foliage is bronzy-red, turning to light green. The creamy-white flowers are carried in loose, erect clusters at branch ends in late spring. Shiny, red berry clusters may follow if the plants are grouped; single plants rarely produce fruit. It does well in shade, but is subject to chlorosis. This is an effective plant for adding vertical interest to a garden, and for small screens, containers, or Japanese gardens. Propagate from seed.

Nasturtium: see *Tropaeolum*

Natal Plum: see *Carissa*

Neem Tree: see *Azederacha*

Nerium oleander

(Oleander)
All zones. This evergreen shrub is one of the most widely grown in the Middle East. It is very hardy and drought-tolerant, and survives salinity levels up to 9,000-10,000 ppm. Growth is moderate to fast, with most varieties reaching 2.5-3.5m (8-12ft) in height and width. Normally a broad and bulky shrub, it can be pruned into a multi-trunk small tree, and one variety, 'Sister Agnes', can be pruned to make a handsome standard (single trunk) tree. The 10-25cm-long (4-10in) narrow leaves are dark green and leathery with a prominent white vein down the centre. Both double and single flower forms are available; 5-8cm (2-3in) across, they are clustered at the end of branches or twigs, with a colour range from white to salmon, pink, and red. Blooms are borne almost all year round.

Oleander thrive in most types of soil and love the heat and full sun. They will grow in shade, but will not flower well.

Oleander should be pruned in early spring to control their size and shape: open up the interior of the plant by cutting out some main stems all the way to the ground. To control height during the growing season, pinch off tips or prune lightly. To prevent bushiness at the base, pull off (do not cut) unwanted sucker growth.

Oleander are somewhat susceptible to brown and black scale and aphids. Control with Malathion or Supracide.

Caution: All parts of the plant are poisonous. Warn children not to eat the leaves or the flowers. Do not use the wood for barbecue fires, as the smoke can cause irritation.

This is an excellent plant for screens or driveway borders or against walls, and as a background planting. It is also attractive in large tubs or planters. White oleander gives a cool look to a garden. Propagate by cuttings.

Varieties include:
   'Cherry Ripe': reddish pink, single
      flowers
   'Hardy Red': large, bright red, single
      flowers in heavy clusters
   'Mrs Roeding': double, salmon pink
      flowers
   'Petite Pink': dwarf shrub (to 1.2m/4ft);
      single, pink flowers
   'Petite Salmon: dwarf; single, bright
      salmon flowers
   'Sister Agnes': single white flowers;
      grows to 6m (20ft) when pruned as a tree.

Night-blooming Jasmine: see *Cestrum*

O

Ocimum basilicum
(Sweet Basil)
Annual herb. All zones. This is a small shrub reaching a height of 60cm (24in), with 5cm (2in) oval, shiny green leaves. Erect, 10-15cm (4-6in) spikes of white or purple flowers are borne. This is an attractive shrub for borders and flower gardens; it is also a useful cooking herb. Fresh leaves are used in salads and stews; dried leaves are used for poultry seasoning, egg dishes, souffles and fish. Propagate from seed.

Oenothera
(Evening Primrose)
Biennials, perennials. All zones. These are unusual plants, in that their flowers, which bloom in summer, open at night.

O. biennis
Biennial. This many-branched plant has green to red stems and yellow flowers. It reaches a height of 1m (3ft).

O. hookeri
Biennial. This reaches a height of 1.5m (5ft). The bright yellow, bowl-shaped flowers are 8cm (3in) diameter.

O. speciosa childsii
(Mexican Evening Primrose)
Perennial. The rose-pink, 3cm (1in) flowers bloom day and night on 30cm (12in) stems. When the blooms fade, the stems die back and need to be pruned to ground level.

Olea europea
(Olive)
Evergreen tree. All zones. Salt-tolerant to 7,000-9,000 ppm. Native to the Mediterranean. This is a picturesque, vigorous tree, particularly when grown as a multi-trunk, reaching 9m (30ft) high and wide. It is fast-growing in early years, slowing down as it matures. The small, oval foliage is glossy green on top, and silvery-grey on the underside. It is bushy when young, so that pruning and training is required early to achieve the shape desired in the mature tree. To shape as a standard tree, prune off all the lower growth except the strongest, straightest stem. Tie this stem to a stake and keep it staked until the self-supporting trunk develops. To shape as a multi-trunk, cut out all stems except the 3 or 4 strongest. Stake these into a balanced, radiating shape. Keep pruning away the lower sucker growth and cut branches regularly to maintain a balanced shape.

Without soil leaching and processing of the olives, the fruits are inedible, and they can be a real nuisance when they start dropping. Fruitless varieties are available but are somewhat unreliable. The interesting branching structure and the pretty foliage make this an attractive tree for courtyards or patios. It is not recommended for lawns because of fruit drop. Propagate from cuttings.

Oleander: see *Nerium*

Oleander, Yellow: see *Thevetia*

Olive: see *Olea*

Onion
Aromatic, strongly flavoured bulb. All zones. Generally, white onions are grown from sets (small bulbs), and red onions from seed. Plant sets 3-4cm (1½in) deep, 3-4cm (1½in) apart. Green onions can be harvested in 3 weeks. Harvest mature, dry onions when the grassy tops wilt after 6-8 weeks. Dig them out of the ground and let them dry for 3-4 days, then cut off the tops and roots and store in a cool dry place. Keep moist while growing.

Opuntia: see **Cactus**

Opuntia microdasys
(Bunny Ears)

Orange-Osteospermum

Osteospermum fruiticosum (Trailing African Daisy)

Orange: see **Citrus**

Orchid Tree: see *Bauhinia*

Oregano: see *Origanum*

Origanum vulgare
(Oregano)
Perennial herb. All zones. This is an upright shrub, reaching 70cm (28in), which spreads by rhizomes. It has 6-8cm-long (2-3in), oval leaves and purplish-pink flowers. The leaves (fresh or dried) are used in many Italian and Spanish dishes. If your plant is to be used for seasoning, keep it pruned to prevent it flowering.

Osteospermum fruiticosum
(Trailing African Daisy)
All zones but 6. Native to southern Africa. Salt-tolerant to 2,000 ppm. This makes an excellent flowering ground cover in the Middle East. It is fast-growing to 30cm (12in) high and 1m (3ft) wide. The deep green, somewhat tongue-shaped, 12cm-long (5in), daisy-like flowers (white with purple centres, lavender, or deep purple) bloom most profusely in winter. The trailing stems root as they spread, making this a good ground cover for banks. Creates an attractive effect spilling over a wall or in hanging baskets. Propagate from cuttings.

Palo Verde-Pelargonium

P

Palo Verde: see *Cercidium*

Pampas Grass: see *Cortaderia*

Papaver nudicaule
(Iceland Poppy)
Perennial grown as an annual. All zones. This is
a small, clumping plant with hairy, divided
leaves. The cup-shaped flowers, 8cm (3in) in
diameter, are carried at the tops of 40-60cm-
long (16-24in), thin, hairy stems. The blooms
range in colour from white to yellow, orange,
salmon, rose and pink. Propagate from seed.

Parkinsonia aculeta
(Jerusalem Thorn)
Arabic: *Seysaban*
Semi-deciduous tree. Native to South America.
Zones 1,3,5,6,7. Salt-tolerant to 9,000 ppm.
Drought-tolerant, but small leaflets tend to drop
during extended dry periods. This is a fast-
growing, vigorous tree reaching 6m (20ft). The
young bark is a bright green colour, turning to
greyish-brown, and the branches are thorny.
The 20-35cm-long (8-14in) leaves have many
tiny leaflets, giving a feathery, fern-like
appearance. The loose clusters of fragrant,
bright yellow flowers make it particularly
attractive during spring. This is a good-looking
tree for courtyards and patios, or scattered
throughout parks, both as a standard or as a
multi-trunk. It does not do well with lawn
watering and requires regular pruning.
Propagate from seed.

Parsley: see *Petroselinum*

Passiflora
(Passion Flower)
Evergreen to decidous vines. Zones 1,3,5,7.
These are vigorous vines that climb by means of
tendrils. They need heavy annual pruning to
keep them from tangling and getting leggy.
They have most unusual, multi-coloured
flowers. They can also be used as a ground
cover. Propagate from seed, cuttings.

P. alato-caerulea
Semi-evergreen. The 8cm-long (3in) leaves are
three-lobed. The fragrant flowers, 8-10cm (3-
4in) in diameter, are white, shaded pink and
lavender with deep blue or purple crowns.
They bloom all summer. This is a plant best
protected from wind.

Parkinsonia aculeta
(Jerusalem Thorn)

P. caerulea
(Blue Crown Passion Flower)
Semi-evergreen. The leaves are five-lobed,
mid-green and smaller than *P. alato-caerulea*.
The flowers, too, are smaller, and greenish
white, with white and purple crowns. They are
followed by small, oval, orange fruit.

Passion Flower: see *Passiflora*

Peepul Tree: see *Ficus*

Pelargonium
(Geranium)
All zones but 6. Shrubby perennial. Flowers best
if given light shade in the summer. All varieties
need a lot (40-50%) of organic material in the
soil to counteract alkalinity. They are also
sensitive to salts in the water. This is a good
plant for flower beds or indoor containers.
Propagate from seed or cuttings.

Pelargonium-Phlox

P. domesticum
(Martha Washington Geranium)
This is an upright plant reaching a height of 90cm (36in), which tends to get rangy and leggy without pruning. The heart-to-kidney-shaped, dark green, 6-10cm-long (2-4in) leaves have crinkled edges. The loose, 5-8cm (2-3in), round flower clusters range in colour from white to pink, red, lavender, and purple; some with markings in darker colours.

P. gravebleus
(Rose Geranium)
Rounded bush to 60cm (24in). The deep green, slightly hairy, deeply lobed leaves have a spicy, rose-like fragrance. The small, modest flowers are rose-coloured or pink-veined and purplish.

P. hortorum
(Common Geranium)
This is a widely grown plant, shrubby, with succulent stems reaching 1m (3½ft) height and spread. Older plants need pruning to prevent them getting woody. The green leaves are round or kidney-shaped and velvety to the touch, with scalloped edges, changing colour inside the edges. Clusters of single or double flowers are borne, ranging in colour from white to pink, rose, red, orange and violet.

P. peltatum
(Ivy Geranium)
Trailing vines or ground cover. The glossy, bright green, ivy-like leaves are 5-8cm (2-3in) long, with pointed lobes. Single or double flowers are borne in colours ranging from white to pink, rose, red and lavender.

Peltaphorum inerme
(Rusty Shieldbearer)
Semi-deciduous tree. Zones 1,3,5,7. Salt-tolerant to 3,000 ppm. This is a good shade tree reaching 20m (67ft) once it is well established, but it needs regular pruning to keep it dense with a balanced crown. Many small leaflets are carried on feathery, bipinnate leaves with the undersides hairy and rust-coloured. Small clusters of yellow flowers appear at the branch ends in spring. The fruit is a pod that eventually turns blackish-brown, and hangs on the tree for months. Propagate from seed.

Pennisetum setaceum
(Fountain Grass)
Arabic: *Halfa-sabat-sabet*
Perennial grass. All zones. Drought-resistant.

The dense, rounded, grassy clumps reach 60cm (24in). In summer, 80-90cm (32-36in), hollow stems are tipped with fuzzy, showy, pink or purplish flower spikes. This is a useful plant for providing contrast in borders or drifts in a flower garden. Feeding 2-3 times a year with a complete fertilizer may prevent it from going dormant in winter. It can be a spreading pest if flower spikes are not cut before they go to seed. Propagate from seed or cutting, or by division.

Pepper, Brazilian: see **Schinus**

Pepper, California: see **Schinus**

Peppermint: see **Mentha**

Petroselinum crispum
(Parsley)
Biennial, but best grown as an annual. All zones: zones 2,4, plant in April; other areas, may be planted all year round. This small plant forms clumps up to 30cm (12in) high, with finely cut, tufted, dark green foliage. This makes a lovely, contrasting edging or border plant for herb or flower gardens. Full sun. Propagate from seed that has been pre-soaked in warm water for 24 hours.

Petunia hybrida
(Petunia)
All zones. Colourful, showy, very popular annual bedding plant. In cold weather areas, petunias should be planted in spring for summer colour; in other areas they can be planted year-round. The thick-ribbed, deep green, elliptical leaves are a little sticky. Slightly scented flowers are borne, single, funnel-shaped or double, in a great variety of colours from white to red to deepest blue and purple. Petunias should be planted 30cm (12in) apart and fertilized monthly with a complete fertilizer. As the flowers fade and the plant starts to get rangy, pinch back halfway to force new growth. This is a superb plant for edging or border use, or in large drifts of colour. Propagate from seed.

Phlox drummondii
(Annual Phlox)
All zones. This is a clumping, colourful bedding plant with leafy, erect stems which have rather sticky hairs. Profuse, showy clusters of flowers are borne on top of the stems. There is a wide range of colours available (but not blue or orange). Grow from seed.

Phoenix

Phoenix dactylifera
(Date Palm)
Arabic: *Nakheel Bala*
All zones. Native to Iraq and the Arabian
peninsula. This is a tall, stately, arching palm
whose fruit has been the lifeblood of Arabia for
centuries. It grows to an overall height of 20m
(67ft), with straight trunks, whose diameter at
the ground can reach 80-100cm (32-40in). The
deep green, arching fronds have long, narrow
leaflets from the base to the tip, and spread to
12m (40ft) in a mature tree. Clusters of small
creamy flowers precede the date fruit. Until the
past few years, this was Saudi Arabia's main
agricultural crop. It is also the largest and most
dominant tree in the Middle Eastern landscape.
One reason for this is that it can be transplanted
with an excellent chance of survival. For best
survival rate, mature trees should be moved
during the warmer months. Transplanting can
be safely carried out if the root ball is double the
size of the trunk diameter, although trees have
survived transplanting with the root ball smaller
than the trunk. All but the inner core of fronds
(ie 8-12) should be cut and tied before moving.
Just prior to planting, wrap the upper tip of the
trunk and the base of the frond in 1-1.5m (3-5ft)
of burlap to protect the sensitive inner 'heart'
where the new fronds sprout. This burlap
should be left on for up to six months or when
new hardy growth is obvious. After planting, all
the fronds may die out, but if planted properly,
this hardy tree will produce new growth up
through the dead fronds within three to five
months. The height of date palms is measured in
'clear trunk' from the ground to the base of the
newer fronds; trees with up to 8m (27ft) of clear
trunk have been safely transplanted. It is
expensive, but if a tree is moved with a 2m
(6½ft) root ball, the fronds do not need
wrapping and the graceful arching effect is
retained.
    Plant in loose soil with good drainage. If you
are planting in a rocky area, use the following
procedure for large specimens. Dig a hole 2m
deep×2m wide (6½×6½ft). Place 30-40cm
(12-16in) of drainage gravel in the bottom. Fill
to the bottom of the root ball with pure dune
sand and compact this with the aid of water.
Place the tree in the hole (you will need a crane
for large trees) so that the top of the root ball is at
ground level. Fill in with a soil mix of 85% dune
sand, 15% organic material (ground tree bark
or peat moss) to 5cm (2in) above soil level to
allow for settling. Make a soil basin around the
tree to hold water. During the warmer months,

(top) *Phoenix dactylifera*
(Date Palm), shortly
after pollination, (left)
Petunia, (below left)
Phlox drummondii
(Annual Phlox)

Phormium-Pinus

irrigate with 100-150 litres of water per day (for larger trees) until the tree is established or the winter rains take over.

It is difficult to get substantial fruit production from a date which is used as a landscape tree. As a crop, trees produce only in groves, with a ratio of 50 female treees to 1 male, and they must be pollinated yearly by hand. Propagation can be effected by chopping off side shoots ('pups') at the base of the trunk, taking care to include part of the root system, or alternatively by growing from seed.

Of the 200 or more commercial varieties available in Saudi Arabia, some of the more common are listed below by region.

> Western: *Anbarra, Berni, Hilwa, Safawai, Sukkaret Yanbu.*
> Central region: *Barhi, Khudari, Nebut Seif, Sakkari, Sefri, Sultani.*
> Eastern Province: *Khalas, Khunezi, Ruzeiz*

Phormium tenax
(New Zealand Flax)
Evergreen perennial. Zones 1,3,5,7. This is a large plant, forming clumps reaching a height of 2.5m (8ft) with tall, narrow, sword-like leaves set in a fan pattern and coloured green to reddish bronze. Brownish-red flower stalks bear many dark red to yellow flowers above the foliage. This is a bold plant for contrast in a large garden and is also useful as a low screen. Propagate from seed or by division.

Photinia
Evergreen shrubs or small trees with attractive foliage and fruit colour. All zones. These are good for screens or planted as background plants. Propagate from cuttings.

P. fraseri
A rounded shrub or multi-trunk tree reaching 3m (10ft). The 5-10cm-long (2-4in) glossy, dark green leaves have light green undersides. New growth is a showy reddish-bronze. 10cm (5in)-diameter clusters of small, flat, white flowers are borne in early spring. This is a good screen or background plant. The cut branches are attractive in flower arrangements.

P. serrulata
(Chinese Photinia)
Broad, dense growth to 10m (33ft), but easily restricted to 3m (10ft) by regular pruning. The deep green, elliptical leaves are up to 20cm (8in) long and have prickly edges. New growth is a bright copper colour; cold weather produces red leaf colour. Cluster of white spring flowers 15cm (6in) in diameter are followed by red berries. Subject to mildew.

Phyla nodiflora
(Lippia)
Perennial ground cover. Zones 1,3,5,6,7. This is a flat, ground-hugging, small-leafed lawn substitute. The 2cm-long (1in) leaves are grey-green; 1cm (½in), round-headed, rose to lilac flowers are borne from spring to autumn. It is dormant and unattractive in winter. Feed with a complete fertilizer in early spring and every two months thereafter.

Pimpinella anisum
(Anise)
This annual herb has bright green, toothed, basal leaves. Umbrella-like clusters of tiny, white flowers are borne on 60cm-high (24in) stems in early summer. The fresh leaves are used in salads, and the seeds can be used for flavouring biscuits and sweets. Propagate from seed.

Pine, Aleppo: see *Pinus*

Pine, Russian: see *Pinus*

Pine, Yew: see *Podocarpus*

Pineapple Guava: see *Feijoa*

Pink Ironbark: see *Eucalyptus*

Pink Jasmine: see *Jasminum*

Pink Melaleuca: see *Melaleuca*

Pinus
(Pine)
Evergreen trees. Conifers (i.e. they produce needles instead of leaves, and the seeds appear in hard brown clusters called pine cones). With the two exceptions below, pines are not well-suited to the high temperatures and alkaline soils of the Middle East. They require very little feeding, and should never be fed with a fertilizer high in nitrogen. They are susceptible to mites and aphids, and require good drainage. Non-flowering. Propagate from seed.

P. elderica
(Russian Pine)
All zones except 6. Drought- and salt-tolerant.

Pinus-Plum

Thought to be native to southern Russia, Afghanistan, and Pakistan, this is perhaps the only pine that survives well in desert areas. It is fairly fast growing to 10-20m (33-66ft), with a dense growth habit, and the classic pyramidal pine shape. 10-15cm-long (4-6in), dark green needles are carried in pairs. The 7-10cm-long (3-4in), oval to oblong cones are reddish to yellow-brown. This is one of the few conifers that will grow in most Middle Eastern areas.

P. halepensis
(Aleppo Pine)
Zones 2,4,7. Drought- and salt-tolerant. Native to Syria and other Eastern Mediterranean areas. This pine is widely used in forestation projects in the hills and mountains of Jordan. With moderate growth to 10-20m (33-66ft), it has a more open and irregular shape that *P. elderica*. The bark is thick and fissured on older specimens. The light green , 6-10cm (2½-4in) needles are usually carried in pairs. Frost tender when young, but older trees will withstand temperatures to −10°C. It will withstand persistent winds, but gets rangy without water. This is a handsome tree if pruned to shape annually while young.

Pithecolobium dulce, also Inge dulce
(Manila Tamarind)
Evergreen tree. Zones 1,3,5.6,7. Salt-tolerant to 2,000 ppm. Native to the Philippines. This is a dense, round-headed, prickly tree reaching 12m (40ft). The dark green leaves have two sets of small, unequal-sided leaflets. Cream flowers are borne in spring, followed by twisted, brownish-red fruit pods. Makes a good shade tree if pruned. Propagate from seed or cuttings.

Plumbago capensis (P. auriculata)
(Cape Plumbago)
Semi-evergreen shrub. All zones but 6. This is a sprawling, mounded bush reaching 3m (10ft) which can be trained as a vine. The light to medium green leaves are 2-5cm (1-2in) long. Flower colour, from white to light blue, varies from plant to plant; flowers appear from mid-spring to mid-winter. It looks best if it is sheltered from summer sun which causes both flowers and leaves to fade. Once established, it requires very little water but needs good drainage. It provides good cover for banks and walls, or is effective as a background plant. Propagate from cuttings.

Plum, Natal: see *Carissa*

(top) *Pithecolobium dulce* (Manila Tamarind), (above) *Plumbago capensis* (Cape Plumbago)

Plumeria-Pongamia

(above) *Poinciana pulcherima* (Barbados Pride), (right) *Plumeria rubra* (Frangipani)

Plumeria
(Frangipani)
Arabic: *Yasmin Hindi*
Evergreen and deciduous shrubs or small trees. Zones 1,5. Need high humidity and are sensitive to frost. They have a round-headed, open-branched appearance and reach 2.5m (8ft). The large, leathery, pointed leaves radiate from the branch tips. The showy, waxy, very fragrant flowers are borne in clusters. Plumeria can provide superb focal points in small gardens or patios. They are easily grown from cuttings.

P. obtusa
(Singapore Plumeria)
Evergreen. The glossy, dark green leaves are 15cm (6in) long and 5cm (2in) wide. 5cm (3in), white flowers are borne during warm weather.

P. rubra
(Frangipani)
Deciduous. The thick, pointed, 20-40cm-long (8-16in) leaves drop in winter or early spring. The 5-7cm (2-3in) flowers, red, lavender or white with yellow centres, are used in the Hawaiian *leis*. Blooms May to November.

Podocarpus macrophylla
(Yew Pine)
Evergreen tree, shrub. All zones but 6, but needs protection from summer sun. This is a dense tree reaching 10m (33ft) but it can be restricted to 3m (10ft) with regular pruning. Also prune to maintain a balanced, even shape. The narrow, 10cm-long (4in) leaves are dark green. A versatile tree, effective as a container plant or espaliered, or as a dense screen. Propagate from seed.

Poinciana (Caesalpinia)
Evergreen and deciduous shrubs. These fast-growing, colourful, feathery shrubs like full sun and deep, infrequent watering. Propagate from seed or cuttings.

P. gilliesii
(Bird of Paradise Bush)
Zones 1,3,5. This is an evergreen shrub or small tree reaching 3m (10ft) with an open, angular, branching habit and finely cut, filmy foliage. Clusters of yellow flowers, adorned with long, bright red stamens, bloom all summer.

P. pulcherima
(Barbados Pride)
Deciduous shrub. Zones 1,3,5. The dense growth reaches 3m (10ft). The dark green leaves have many 2cm-long (1in) leaflets and the clustered orange or red flowers have red stamens. This is a good tree for a small garden.

Pomegranate: see Punica

Pongamia glabra
(Pongam)
Semi-deciduous tree. Zones 1,3,5,7. This is a slow-growing, round-headed tree reaching 8m (27ft). The large, shiny, 12cm-long (5in), deep green and oval leaves have pointed tips. The large clusters of small, white, pea-like flowers in the spring are followed by seed pods. This is an attractive broad-leafed tree for parks and large gardens. It needs pruning to maintain an even crown. Propagate from seed.

Poplar-Prosopis

Poplar: see *Populus*

Poppy: see *Papaver*

Populus
(Poplar)
Deciduous tree. All zones, but thrives best in 2,3 and 4. Poplars are very fast growing and the two species listed here are columnar to pyramid-shaped. They tolerate almost any kind of soil but their roots are invasive, making them unsuitable for planting in lawns or positioning near walls or paving.

P. candicans
(Balm of Gilead)
This tree, which reaches a height of 18m (60ft), is generally narrow when young, but the crown broadens out as it matures. It produces suckers in profusion. The triangular leaves are up to 15cm (6in) long and 10cm (4in) wide.

P. nigra 'Italica'
(Lombardy Poplar)
This is a beautiful, tall, narrow tree that can reach 30m (100ft). It produces suckers in profusion. The bright green, 10cm-long (4in), triangular leaves turn golden yellow in the autumn. This columnar, stately tree can be found bordering many roads and country driveways in Europe.

Portulaca grandiflora
(Rose Moss, Sun Plant)
Annual. All zones. Drought-tolerant, but more attractive with regular watering. This is a bright flowering ground cover with fleshy, reddish-brown stems. The succulent, cylindrical, pointed leaves are 3cm (1in) long. Lustrous, rose-like, small flowers are borne in bright red, pink, orange, yellow and white. Propagate from seed.

Pot Marigold: see *Calendula*

Pride of Madeira: see *Echium*

Prosopis
(Mesquite)
Evergreen tree. All zones. Drought-tolerant. These are fine-leafed, true desert trees that thrive in the hot sun and tolerate alkaline soils. They provide shade in deserts throughout the world. Propagate from seed.

P. juliflora (P. chinesis)
Native to the south-west USA. Salt-tolerant to 25,000 ppm. This is a wide-spreading, drooping, heavily branched tree with a shapely, airy, umbrella-shaped crown. It reaches 10m (35ft) high and 12m (40ft) wide. The bipinnate leaves have small, linear, oblong leaflets. The early spring foliage is a bright emerald green, turning to a blueish green. Sparse, hanging, cylindrical spikes of small yellow flowers are borne in spring followed by flat, curled, pale yellow seed pods. The stems are thorny. This is a fast grower which requires staking and frequent pruning to train as a standard shade tree: it is used extensively as a street tree. The wood is renowned as a charcoal for flavouring barbecued meats.

P. spicigera
Native to the Arabian peninsula. Salt-tolerant to 4,500 ppm. A slow-growing tree, but eventually reaching 20m (67ft), with a grey, fissured bark and thorny stems. The dense, feathery, pendant foliage consists of small leaflets that drop frequently. The bright yellow, showy spring flowers are followed by small, slightly curved, tannish-brown seed pods. Mature specimens are quite handsome when used in a desert garden setting.

Prosopis juliflora
(Mesquite)

Punica-Quisqualis

Punica granatum
(Pomegranate)

Punica granatum
(Pomegranate)
Deciduous shrub or tree. All zones, but protect against heavy frost in zones 2 and 4. Salt-tolerant to 7,000 ppm. Likes full sun, any soil. This is an upright shrub or small tree reaching 4m (13ft) with spiny branches. The small, narrow, glossy leaves are bronze-coloured when young, turning to a bright or golden green. Orange-red, single flowers, up to 10cm-long (4in), are carried at the end of shoots in the summer. The reddish-brown fruit, resembling a small apple, is carried in the early autumn. Pomegranates need deep, regular watering in order to produce a good fruit crop. This makes a good background plant or natural hedge. Dwarf, compact varieties are available, as are varieties with creamy-white, yellow or double flowers. Propagate from seed or cuttings.

Purple Orchid Tree: see *Bauhinia*

Q

Queen Palm: see *Cocos*

Quisqualis indica
(Red Jasmine)
Evergreen vine or climbing shrub. Zones 1,3,5,7. The light green, oval leaves are downy. The beautiful, drooping, very fragrant flowers have petals that are white when opening, changing to pink and then crimson red. This is a colourful vine. Propagate from cuttings.

R

Railway Creeper: see *Ipomoea*

Red Gum: see *Eucalyptus*

Red Jasmine: see *Quisqualis*

Red Sandalwood: see *Adenanthera*

Rhus lancia
(African Sumac)
Evergreen tree. All zones. This tree has a graceful, round-headed, weeping growth habit, reaching 7m (23ft). The leaves are divided into 3 willow-like, narrow, 10cm-long (4in) leaflets. Female trees bear clusters of pea-like, yellow or red summer fruit. This is a versatile tree that can be pruned as a standard or multi-trunk, with interesting branch patterns and red, fissured bark. It can be used for screens or clipped hedges but is most attractive as a focal point in small gardens. Propagate from seed or cuttings.

Ricinus communis
(Castor Bean)
Annual to biennial. All zones. This is a bold, umbrella-shaped or round-headed shrub or small tree, reaching 5m (17ft). The large, deeply lobed, dark green (sometimes purplish) leaves reach 30cm (12in) in length. Loose clusters of small, greenish-white flowers are borne on 30cm (12in) stalks in winter, followed in spring by prickly, chestnut-type fruits containing smooth, dark seeds. These seeds are highly poisonous, indeed fatal. Also the leaves can cause contact allergies, so avoid planting where children play. *Ricinus* is grown commercially for castor oil extracted from seeds. Experiments are being conducted in genetic engineering, using the poison Ricin to combat cancer.

Robinia pseudocacia
(Black Locust)
Deciduous tree. All zones, but subject to heat stress during hot summers. Tolerant of drought and of alkaline soil. This tree enjoys rapid growth, reaching 20m (67ft) with an open, sparse-branching habit. It has deeply furrowed, light brown bark and thorny branchlets. The leaves are divided into 7-19, 4cm-long (2in) leaflets. Dense, hanging clusters of small, white fragrant flowers are borne in summer. The 10 cm-long (4in), brown, bean-like pods are carried throughout the winter. The roots are invasive. Propagate from seed.

Rockrose: see *Cistus*

(above) *Rosa* (Rose),
(left) *Ricinus communis*
(Castor Bean)

Rosa
(Rose)
Deciduous to semi-evergreen, bushy or climbing shrubs. All zones. The rose is perhaps the most widely planted garden shrub in the world. There are many types of roses, but by far the most popular are the hybrid teas. These are the large, spectacular flowers in a myriad of colours on dark-leafed shrubs 1-1.5m (3-5ft) high and wide. Climbing roses are also popular as a covering for walls, trellises or arbors, up to a height of 3-10m (10-33ft) or more. Some people favour the polyanthas (1.8×1.2m/9×6ft high and wide) or floribundas (1.5×1m/5×3ft high and wide) which generally have smaller flowers in clusters and very little fragrance. Grandiflora types have flowers similar to hybrid teas but are

127

Rosa

Rosa (Rose)

much larger shrubs which reach 3m (10ft). Some varieties are valuable for their cut flowers. And many gardeners like the miniatures – 15-30cm (6-12in) shrubs, with small but profuse blooms. If you are just starting with roses, I would recommend the hybrid teas. You will have a wealth of colours and sizes to choose from both for cut flowers and the garden.

To grow roses successfully, remember these rules:

1. Buy only top grade, healthy plants suitable for your climate and buy 'bare root' in December-February.

2. Locate and plant them properly.

3. Provide properly the four basics: water; fertilizer; pruning; pest and disease control.

Roses will grow well in almost any arid or temperate climate but to produce the maximum flowering in the Middle East, most varieties need to be sheltered from the summer afternoon sun. The best solution is to grow them on the east side of a building or wall. If that is not possible, try a light, temporary, partial shade structure.

When planting your 'bare root' roses, use a soil mix that is 50% dune sand and 50% ground bark or peat moss, and mix in a complete fertilizer and superphosphate. (See pp. 64-5).

Dig a hole at least 50cm×50cm (20×20in). Fill the hole approximately two-thirds full with the soil mixture, and moisten. After cutting back any dead or broken stems and roots of the plant, carefully place the roots into the soil so that the bud union is lightly above ground level. Fill in the hole and firmly tamp down the soil mixture to remove air pockets. Build a soil basin around the plant, then water thoroughly.

Roses like plenty of water, but do not keep the soil saturated or you will encourage root diseases. Let the top 5cm (2in) of soil dry out between waterings. If you irrigate with overhead sprinklers, do it at night so that the stems and foliage are dry during the day.

Always keep a 5-8cm (2-3in) layer of mulch around the plant, preferably ground bark. This helps keep the soil moist and cool in the summer, and will keep weed growth down and build a healthy soil structure.

Start fertilizing with a complete fertilizer in February or when new growth starts after winter dormancy. Thereafter, feed approximately once a month. Ideally, however, the best time to fertilize is when a blooming period has come to an end and new growth is starting for the next blooming period.

Pruning is vitally important for successful roses, so follow these rules:

1. Heavy pruning should only be done once a year at the end of the dormant period when new buds start to appear. Cut the plant back to one-half or one-third of its size to give it a nice even shape, preferably always to an outward-pointing bud.

2. Regularly remove all wood that is dead, broken, sun-scalded, or covered with lesions.

3. Remove any centre-pointing branches that cross or rub each other.

4. Remove all lower sucker growth, particularly those that grow out of the soil. Cut these slightly below ground level.

5. Let the stems grow long enough so that when you are pruning for cut flowers you will have enough stem for a vase, yet still leave at least two sets of five-leaflet leaves below a healthy bud.

Rosemary-Rusty Shieldbearer

6. Always cut about 1cm (½in) above a leaf node and down to the third or fourth from the end of the stem.

For all the beauty roses provide, there is a price to pay. They need constant care and attention to keep them healthy and to maximize flower production. Part of this price is control of the numerous pests and diseases to which roses are susceptible. Aphids, thrips, scale, and spider mites are all insects that are attracted to them. Similarly, white powdery mildew, found on the upper surface of leaves, and rust, found on the underside, are two types of fungus you may encounter (see p. 67 for treatment). Chlorosis (yellowing of the leaves) should be treated with iron chelate or iron sulphate. Each 'bare root' season (December-February), most nurseries and flower shops offer a wide selection of roses: those from Holland or the United States are generally the highest quality. Buy these, follow the recommendations given above, and your world should be a brighter and rosier one.

Rosmarinus officinalis
(Rosemary)

Rosemary: see *Rosmarinus*

Rose Moss: see *Portulaca*

Rosmarinus officinalis
(Rosemary)
Arabic: *Hasa Leban*
Evergreen shrub, ground cover, and herb. All zones. Drought-tolerant. This is a popular, wide-spreading ground cover in the Middle East, but some varieties, which reach 1.5m (5ft), can also be used as shrubs or as a clipped hedge. The small, narrow, needle-like leaves are aromatic. Clusters of 1cm-long (½in), lavender-blue flowers bloom off and on throughout the year. Rosemary can provide a lovely effect cascading over low walls. The dried leaves provide a versatile seasoning in cooking.

Royal Poinciana: see *Delonix*

Rusty Shieldbearer: see *Peltaphorum*

Sage-Schinus

S

(above) *Sanseveria trifasciata* (Mother-in-Law's Tongue), (right) *Schinus molle* (California Pepper)

Sage: see *Salvia*

Sago Palm: see *Cycas*

Salt Bush: see *Atriplex*

Salvia
(Sage)
Annuals and perennials. All zones. Sages are characterized by flowers in whorls, sometimes separate, sometimes so close together that they appear as one dense spike. Colours range from deep blue to purple to bright scarlet. The two species below are the most popular.

S. officinalis
(Garden Sage)
Perennial herb. Reaches 60cm (24in) high with narrow, grey-green, 3-5cm (1-2in) leaves. Tall spikes of violet-blue flowers appear in early summer, and should be cut back after bloom. Plants should be divided every 2-4 years. Propagate from seed or cuttings, or by division.

S. splendens
(Scarlet Sage)
Annual. This is an upright plant reaching 30-80cm (12-32in) high, depending on variety, with dark green, oval leaves. Brilliant red flowers are borne in clusters at the top of the foliage, from late spring until autumn. It likes full sun but will also flower in partial shade. This is an excellent annual if you want a vivid red as part of your colour scheme. Propagate from seed.

Sanseveria
Evergreen perennials. Zones 1,3,5, but will fade and possibly die in midday sun. They should be grown on the east or north sides of walls or buildings, or as house plants. They thrive in shade and will tolerate low light conditions indoors. Sanseveria occasionally produce erect, narrow clusters of small, greenish-white, fragrant flowers. They are drought-tolerant and will grow in any soil. Propagate by division.

S. hahnii
The broad, fleshy, 15cm-long (6in), dark green leaves are cross-banded with irregular silvery markings. The leaves radiate from the centre, one on top of the other, until the plant reaches 30cm (12in).

S. trifasciata
(Mother-in-Law's Tongue)
This plant reaches 1m (3ft) high, forming clumps of tall, narrow, sword-like, fleshy, dark green leaves which are banded in silver-grey. This is a good contrast plant for tropical gardens, or in pots.

Santolina chamaecyparissus
(Lavender Cotton)
Evergreen perennial herb. All zones. This is a small shrub that will reach 60cm (24in) but looks best if kept pruned to 30cm (12in). Brittle, woody stems carry dense, rough, finely cut, whitish-grey leaves. The bright yellow, button-like flowers bloom in summer. The leaves are fragrant when crushed. This makes a good border or foreground plant, or ground cover. Propagate from seed.

Scarlet Cordia: see *Cordia*

Schinus
(Pepper Tree)
These handsome evergreen trees can be dramatic in a landscape but, at the same time, create a messy clean-up problem because of their fruit drop.

Schinus-Sycamore Fig

S. molle
(California Pepper)
Arabic: *Felfel*
All zones. Salt-tolerant to 5,000 ppm. This fast-growing, round-headed tree reaches 12m (40ft) and has a graceful, weeping, pendulous appearance. The trunks of old specimens are heavily gnarled with rough, light brown bark. The bright green leaves are divided into many small, narrow, 5cm-long (2in) leaflets. Inconspicuous, yellow-white flowers are followed by red, pepper-sized berries. This is an informal tree for large gardens and parks, but its usefulness is reduced by the litter problem. It can also be used for screens or large hedges. Propagate from seed or cuttings.

S. terebinthifolia
(Brazilian Pepper)
Zones 1,3,5,7. Salt-tolerant to 3,000 ppm. This tree has a moderate growth rate up to a height of 10m (33ft). It has a round-headed to umbrella-shaped crown with dark green, glossy, elliptical leaves that are larger (to 8cm/3in) than *S. molle*, with only 7 leaflets per leaf. The flowers are insignificant, but bright red, showy berries are borne in winter. This is a good street or park tree as a standard (single trunk), but is most striking as a wide-spreading multi-trunk. It is excellent as the focal point of a large garden. To reduce the possibility of wind damage, shorten overlong horizontal branches and thin the interior of the tree periodically to allow the wind to pass through. Propagate from cuttings.

Sea Lavender: see *Limonium*

Senecio cineraria
(Dusty Miller)
Arabic: *Fidhiah*
All zones. This is a round, clumping plant reaching 60cm (24in). The long, white to silvery-white leaves are cut into many, blunt-tipped lobes. Clusters of yellow to creamy-yellow flowers are borne at various times of the year. If the plant gets leggy, cut it back to one-half or one-third of its size. This is perhaps the most notable and striking of the grey foliage plants, providing dramatic effects in a border or as clumps scattered throughout a ground cover area. Propagate from seed or by division.

Sesbania aegyptica
(Sesban)
Evergreen shrub, tree. Zones 1,3,5,7. Salt-tolerant to 8,000 ppm. This is a very fast-growing, short-lived, rangy shrub or small tree. The bipinnate leaves have many oblong leaflets. Yellow, pea-like flowers, sometimes tinged with purple, are borne in spring, followed by long, narrow seed pods. This is a useful plant where an immediate screen or filler plant is needed. It can reach 2m (6ft) from seed in one year.

Shamel Ash: see *Fraxinus*

Silk Tree: see *Albizzia*

Silverberry: see *Eleagnus*

Singapore Plumeria: see *Plumeria*

Smoke Tree: see *Cotinus*

Snapdragon: see *Antirrhinum*

Spanish Dagger: see *Yucca*

Spanish Lavender: see *Lavandula*

Spearmint: see *Mentha*

Statice: see *Limonium*

Stenolobium: see *Tecoma*

Strawflower: see *Helichrysum*

Summer Cypress: see *Kochia*

Sunflower: see *Helianthus*

Sweet Alyssum: see *Lobularia*

Sweet Marjoram: see *Marjorana*

Sycamore Fig: see *Ficus*

Senecio cineraria (Dusty Miller)

Tagetes-Tecoma

T

(above) *Tecoma stans* (Yellow Trumpet Flower), (right) *Tagetes erecta* (African Marigold)

Tagetes
(Marigold)
Annuals. All zones. These are strong, vigorous plants that will provide a profusion of bright, warm colours for 9 or 10 months of the year. Fast growing from seed, with delicate, fern-like, deeply lobed foliage, they make long-lasting cut flowers. Two distinct types are available:

T. erecta
(American, African Marigolds)
A broad variety with plants from 20cm (8in) dwarfs to 1m-high (3ft) bushes. These include the big, puffy, double marigolds with flowers up to 12cm (5in) in diameter, in varying shades of yellow and orange. They are notable for their effect of almost solid colour.

T. patula
(French Marigold)
These are generally smaller plants and flowers than *T. erecta*. The shrublets range in size from 15 to 40cm (6-16in), the blooms from 2 to 5cm (1-2in). The single or double flowers range in colour from yellow to rich brownish maroon, with many bicolours.

Tamarix
(Tamarisk)
All zones. Salt-tolerant to 20,000 ppm. These are hardy, vigorous, conifer-like trees that are widely used in the Middle East as windbreaks and screens. They are very drought-tolerant and will survive the harshest desert conditions.

T. aphylla (articulata)
(Athel Tree)
This upright, rangy tree reaches 10m (33ft) high and 6m (20ft) wide. It has greyish-green foliage consisting of minute leaves. Pink spikes of spring flowers are carried at the end of shoots, followed by the capsule-like fruit. This is a sturdy, utilitarian plant for informal effects.

T. pentandra
(Salt Cedar)
Very similar to *T. aphylla*, but somewhat smaller, with more feathery foliage. The pale pink flowers appear in summer. This can be an attractive shrub which flowers profusely, providing it is severely pruned every spring. It is easily propagated from large or small cuttings or from seed.

Tangerine: see *Citrus*

Tarragon: see *Artemesia*

Tecoma stans (stenolobium stans)
(Yellow Trumpet Flower)
Arabic: *Alsafra*
Evergreen shrub, small tree. Zones 1,3,5,7. Salt-tolerant to 3,000 ppm. This is a strongly branched, somewhat untidy shrub that needs

Tecomaria-Thevetia

regular pruning to maintain a balanced, dense shape. It makes an attractive, multi-trunk tree. The deep green leaves have 5-11, lance-shaped leaflets with saw-toothed edges. Tight clusters of bright yellow, trumpet-shaped flowers are borne at the ends of the branchlets in early spring. The fruit resemble long, slender capsules. This is a highly decorative plant, good for screening or as an individual tree in a small garden. Propagate from seed or cuttings.

Tecomaria capensis
(Cape Honeysuckle)
Evergreen shrub or vine. Zones 1,3,5,7. Native to southern Africa. This is an upright shrub reaching 2.5m (8ft), if pruned regularly. As a vine it will grow to a height of 7m (23ft), but it needs support. The leaves are divided into many dark green, glossy, fine-textured leaflets. Vivid orange-red, tubular flowers are borne in tight clusters, from autumn through to spring. This makes an attractive filler shrub. Propagate from cuttings.

Terminalia catappa
(Indian Almond)
Semi-deciduous tree. Zones 1,3,5,7. Salt-tolerant to 4,500 ppm. Reaching a height of 18m (60ft), this tree has a horizontal branching structure that sometimes produces a layered effect. The large, leathery, oval leaves, which are up to 30cm (12in) long are produced in clusters at the branch ends. Creamy, pale yellow flowers spikes are followed by oval, green nuts. This is an excellent shade tree, and one of the few large-leafed trees suitable for desert areas. The continuous leaf drop can be a clean-up problem. It requires space, so is suited to large gardens or parks, and takes a while to establish itself, but once well-rooted, it grows quickly. However, it is difficult to grow any ground cover within its deep shade. Propagate from seed.

Teucrium chamaedrys
(Germander)
Evergreen ground cover. All zones. This is a dense, low-growing, 30cm-high (12in) plant, spreading to 60cm (24in), with numerous woody stems. It has small, toothed, dark green leaves. Loose spikes of reddish-purple or white flowers are borne in spring and summer. It is useful as a foreground plant, in borders, or as ground cover. Propagate from seed or cuttings.

Texas Sage: see **Leucophyllum**

Thespesia populnea
(Aden Apple)
Evergreen tree. Zones 1,5,7. Salt-tolerant to 6,000 ppm. This is a small tree reaching 9m (30ft) with a dense crown of dark green, shiny foliage. The heart-shaped leaves, tapering at the tip, are up to 10cm (4in) long. Short-lived, bell-shaped, yellowish-orange flowers with purple centres are followed by apple-shaped, flattened, fruit capsules. This is an ideal tree for patios, or small gardens, but it needs regular pruning to keep a pleasing shape. Propagate from seed or cuttings.

Thevetia
Evergreen shrubs or small trees. Zones 1,3,5,7. These are narrow-leafed plants with funnel-shaped, yellow or apricot flowers. The leaves and stems are poisonous. Propagate from cuttings.

T. peruviana (nerifolia)
(Yellow Oleander)
Salt-tolerant to 7,000 ppm. This is a dense shrub reaching 3m (10ft) with narrow, 10-12cm-long (4-5in) leaves. The trumpet-shaped, fragrant flowers, which bloom in spring and summer, are a most unusual apricot colour, and are followed by small, apple-shaped fruit. This is a good background plant or a specimen multi-trunk in a small garden.

(top) *Thevetia peruviana* (Yellow Oleander), (above) *Terminalia catappa* (Indian Almond)

Thevetia-Trumpet Flower

Tropaeolum majus
(Nasturtium)

T. thevetioides
(Giant Thevetia)
A fast grower, reaching 4m×4m (13×13ft).
The leaves are darker than *T. peruviana*, and
resemble those of oleander but are corrugated,
with white, downy undersides. Large clusters
of bright yellow flowers are borne from late
spring to winter. A good plant for screens.

Thyme: see *Thymus*

Thymus
(Thyme)
Arabic: *Za'ater*
Ground covers, perennial herbs. All zones.
These are heavily scented foliage plants that like
full sun and well-drained soil. Propagate from
spring cuttings or seed.

T. herba-barona
(Caraway Thyme)
This fast-growing, flat, ground cover has tiny,
caraway-scented leaves. The rose-pink flowers
are borne in summer in rounded, head-like
clusters. The leaves can be used in vegetable
dishes.

T. serpyllum
(Creeping Thyme)
This is a flat ground cover with some upright
branches reaching 15cm (6in). The tiny,
round, dark green, aromatic leaves are
sometimes used in potpourris. Rounded
clusters of tiny, purplish-white flowers are
borne on short stems.

T. vulgaris
(Common Thyme)
This shrubby perennial reaches a height of
30cm (12in). The small, narrow to oval leaves
are grey-green. Tiny lilac flowers are borne in
dense whorls during summer. This is the
commercial thyme. The leaves (fresh or dried)
are used in vegetable juices, soups, seafood,
and poultry stuffing.

Tiger Aloe: see *Aloe*

Tree Aloe: see *Aloe*

Tropaeolum majus
(Nasturtium)
Perennial grown as an annual. All zones. There
are two types: climbing plants that spread over
the ground or climb to 2m (6ft) by means of
coiling leaf stalks; and dwarf, compact types to
40cm (16in). Both have round, shield-shaped
leaves on long stalks, and broad flowers with a
sharp fragrance in creamy-white, yellow,
orange, red, and maroon. The flavour of the
young leaves and the flowers adds interest to a
salad. Nasturtiums provide good, quick colour
for beds and containers. Propagate from seed.

Trumpet Flower, Yellow: see *Tecoma*

U

Ulmus parvifolia
(Chinese Evergreen Elm)
Evergreen to semi-deciduous tree. All zones.
This is a fast-growing, generally round-headed
tree reaching 20m (60ft) or more. Most of the
time it will stay evergreen through the winter,
but a sudden cold snap may cause it to lose its
leaves for a short time. The leathery, oval, 3-6cm
(1-2in) leaves have toothed edges.
Inconspicuous clusters of tiny, white flowers are
borne in early summer, followed by small, dark,
round fruit in the autumn. It makes a useful
street tree or large shade tree for parks.
Propagate from cuttings.

Umbrella Plant: see *Cyperus*

V

Verbena
Zones 1,3,5,7. These perennials are usually
grown as annuals. They are fast-growing
ground covers that provide colourful blooms in
spring and summer, are drought-resistant and
like full sun. Propagate from seed.

V. hybrida
(Garden Verbena)
This many-branched plant reaches 30cm
(12in) high, 80cm (32in) wide. The 6-10cm
(2-4in) leaves are green or grey-green, with
toothed edges. The flat, compact clusters of
flowers are available in a range of colours, from
white to pink, red, purple, blue and
combinations. Water infrequently but deeply
to avoid mildew.

V. peruviana
This is a very flat, spreading ground cover with
small, closely set leaves. A profusion of flat-
topped flower clusters are borne on slender
stems. The most popular colour is a rich scarlet
with a white centre, but hybrids are available
in pink, salmon, purple and white.

Vinca rosea: see *Catharanthus*

Vitex agnus-castus
(Chaste Tree)
Semi-deciduous shrub or small tree. All zones.
This is a wide-spreading tree reaching 7m (23ft)
which can be kept as a dense shrub with
pruning, but is most attractive as a multi-trunk
tree. The leaves are divided into 5-7 narrow,
10-15cm (4-6in) leaflets that are dark green
above, with grey undersides. Showy, upright
spikes of lavender-blue flowers are borne on top
of the foliage in summer and autumn. It can
provide a dramatic focal point for small gardens,
or can be used as a colourful screen.

Washingtonia-Xylosma

W

Washingtonia robusta
(Mexican Fan Palm)

Washingtonia
(Palm)
Arabic: *Nakheel Washingtonia*
Zones 1,3,5,6,7. Drought-tolerant, salt-tolerant to 20,000 ppm. These palms have bold foliage with fan-shaped leaves at the end of spiny, heavy stalks. Propagate from seed.

W. filifera
(California Fan Palm)
Native to southern California, USA. This is a slow-growing palm, reaching 15m (50ft), with a thick knobby trunk. The fan-shaped, deep green, pleated leaves extend up to 2m (6ft) from the trunk (including the stalk). Dead leaves hang down to form a skirt around the upper trunk. The loose white flowers are followed by black fruit. This is a good tropical tree to grow singly in lawn areas or in close groupings in parks or large gardens.

W. robusta
(Mexican Fan Palm)
Similar to *W. filifera*, but faster growing and reaching 30m (100ft). *W. robusta* has slightly shorter leaf stalks with a distinguishing red streak on the undersides and a more slender trunk. It looks effective lining a driveway.

Wattle, Blue Leaf: see *Acacia*

Wattle, Green: see *Acacia*

Willow Acacia: see *Acacia*

Willow, Australian: see *Geijera*

Willow, Desert: see *Chilopsis*

Wormwood: see *Artemesia*

X

Xylosma congestum
Evergreen to semi-deciduous shrub or small tree. All zones but 6. This is a loose, graceful, round-headed shrub that can become ungainly if not pruned. It normally reaches 2.5-3m (8-10ft), but with staking and pruning, it can make an attractive tree up to 7m (23ft) high. The long, pointed, oval leaves are shiny and pale green, with distinctive, bronzy new growth. It is very versatile, being equally happy as an espalier, a clipped hedge or a filler plant. It can be propagated from cuttings, but this is difficult.

Yellow Oleander-Zizyphus

Y

Yellow Oleander: see *Thevetia*

Yellow Trumpet Flower: see *Tecoma*

Yew Pine: see *Podocarpus*

Yucca
These are evergreen, succulent-like perennials with thick, pointed, sword-shaped leaves, and clusters of whitish flowers. Propagate from seed.

Y. aliofolia
Sometimes sold as *Y. gloriosa*
(Spanish Dagger)
Zones 1,3,5. Native to southern USA. This is a slow-growing plant, reaching 3m (10ft) with a single or branching trunk. The dark green, stiff, spine-tipped leaves are up to 80cm (32in) long and 8cm (3in) wide. Variegated forms are also available. Dense, erect clusters of white flowers, sometimes tinted with purple, appear in summer. This makes a picturesque plant, useful for providing a contrast or in desert gardens. The sharp tips of the leaves can be dangerous to children.

Y. filamentosa
(Adam's Needle)
Zones 1,3,5,6,7. This is a stemless plant with 80cm-long (32in) leaves, 3cm (1in) wide, some drooping. Narrow clusters of white flowers are borne on 1.5-2m-long (5-6ft), branching stalks.

Y. whipplei
(Candle Yucca)
Zones 1,35,6,7. This is a stemless plant, with dense clusters of 30-50cm-long (12-20in), rigid, grey-green leaves. They are needle-tipped, and should not be planted where children might run into them. The tall flowering stems, 2-4m (6½-13ft) high, bear branching spikes of drooping, bell-shaped, creamy-white flowers. The plant dies after blooming and producing seed. Propagate from seed or cuttings.

Z

Zizyphus
Evergreen to semi-deciduous trees. All zones. Salt-tolerant to at least 9,000 ppm.

Z. jujuba
(Jujube)
This is a spiny, somewhat ungainly tree reaching 10m (33ft). It can make an attractive, dense shade tree with regular pruning. The glossy, bright green, oval leaves, up to 7cm (3in) long, have three prominent white veins radiating from their base, and pale green undersides. The small, greenish-yellow spring flowers are followed by fleshy, reddish-brown, berry-like fruit. It withstands drought and poor soil conditions, and is commonly used as a street tree. It is, however, susceptible to black scale. Propagate from seed.

Z. spina-christi
Arabic: *Sidr-Nabaq*
This is similar to *Z. jujuba*, but generally smaller. The leaves have a fuzzy surface and the veins are less noticeable.

Zizyphus jujuba
(Jujube)

GLOSSARY OF GARDENING TERMS

A

Acid/alkaline soil Acidity or alkalinity of soils is a description of the concentration of hydrogen ions in the soil. They are expressed, or measured, by a pH (hydrogen) factor. A pH of 7 is neutral; a lower pH indicates acid soil, whilst a higher pH indicates alkaline soil.

Generally, areas of high rainfall, such as India, will have acid soil, whilst those with low rainfall, such as Saudi Arabia, will have alkaline soil. To neutralise acid soils, lime is used; to treat alkaline soils, peat moss, ground bark, or soil sulphur will help increase acidity. Most plants grow best in near neutral soil.

Annual A plant that grows from seed, flowers and dies within a year. Most flowering bedding plants such as marigolds, celosia and zinnias are annuals.

B

Bare root When deciduous plants are dug out of the ground, and the soil is cleaned off the roots for transplanting during the winter dormant season, they are 'bare-rooted'. The roots must be kept moist by placing them in wood shavings or sand, or by wrapping them in plastic bags. Roses are sold this way in January and February.

Biennial Plants grown from seed whose life cycle ends the second year. During mild winters, petunias and sweet william are biennials.

Bipinnate A leaf structure where small, 8-20cm (3-8in) branchlets come off a branch. Each branchlet is actually a leaf, with 15-30 small leaflets on it. Many of the more common desert trees are bipinnate. Examples are *Acacia farnesiana*, *Delonix regia*, and *Albizzia lebbeck*.

Bonsai The Japanese art of training, shaping, and pruning plants in containers to create a miniaturized garden.

Bract Flower part. Modified leaves that grow in a cluster around the flower, and in some plants, such as bougainvillaea, provide the 'flower' colour.

Broad-leafed This refers to plants with wide leaves, as opposed to conifers with needle-like leaves. Also a term used for weeds other than grasses.

Budding A method of propagation, similar to grafting, where the bud of one plant is inserted into a bark opening of another plant. It will maintain the characteristics of the plant from which the bud was taken, and feed on the plant into which it was inserted.

Bulb A thickened underground stem, generally rounded, that has scales or leaves to protect the plant inside. Different from corms, rhizomes, and tubers. Lilies, tulips, and onions are bulbs.

C

Calyx The outer, protective part of a flower, consisting of sepals, which are fused together when the plant is in bud.

Cambium layer The circles of plant tissue, just inside the bark, from which the inner wood and bark of a stem originate their growth.

Chelate (pronounced 'key-late'). A chemical, combining Iron (or Zinc) and an organic substance, which frees the Iron in the soil to be available to plants.

Chlorosis A lack of Iron (or occasionally Zinc or Manganese) in a plant. The symptom is yellow leaves with noticeable green veins. Treat with Iron Chelate (see above).

Composite flowers A family of plants (*Compositae*), including daisies and sunflowers, in which the flower structure is a composite of many minute 'disk' flowers tightly grouped on the centre head, and surrounded by 'ray' flowers. The ray flowers are easily mistaken for petals. Dahlias, marigolds, and marguerites are examples.

Conifer Sometimes called 'evergreens', these are plants with needle-like foliage such as junipers, cypresses, pines, and cedars. All bear cones or cone-like seed structures.

Corm A type of thickened underground stem, similar to a bulb. It differs from the true bulb in that food is stored in the central tissue, not in the scale covering. Gladioli and croci are corms.

Cuttings A method of propagating some plants by causing a section cut from the stem of the plant to develop roots of its own.

D

Damping off A fungus disease in the soil that causes seedlings to rot and die just before or shortly after they break through the soil.

Deciduous A plant that loses its leaves once a year, in most cases during the winter.

Division A method of propagating perennials, bulbs, and other plants that grow in clumps.

Double flower A flower with a large number of overlapping petals that usually hide the inner flower parts.

Drainage The rate at which water passes downward through the soil.

Drip line An imaginary line on the ground directly below the outermost tips of a tree's branches, all the way around the tree.

Dust Some insecticides and fungicides are manufactured as a fine powder. They usually come in a compressible type of container, so that when it is squeezed dust is propelled onto the plant or ground.

E

Epiphyte A type of plant that grows on another plant, but receives no nourishment from it, such as epiphytic orchids.

Espalier A tree or shrub trained to grow in a flat pattern on a trellis or fence.

Evergreen A plant that retains its leaves all year round. Also see *Conifer*.

Everlastings Flowers that hold their shape and colour when dried, such as strawflowers.

Eye An undeveloped growth bud which will produce a new plant or new growth. The 'eye' of a potato is an example, and 'eyes' at the joints of rooted cuttings will produce new growth.

F

Family see **Plant Classification.**

Forcing Increasing the plant's growth beyond its natural rate. Sometimes achieved throuth increased fertilizer application; in other cases, such as commercially grown chrysanthemums and azaleas, flowering is accelerated by varying the amount of light.

Fronds The foliage of ferns and palms.

G

Genus see **Plant classification**.

Grafting A method of propagation, in which a stem (scion) of one plant is inserted into a branch or trunk of another plant (stock).

H

Hardy Frost- or cold-tolerant.

Heading back A method of pruning where a branch is cut back to just above a lateral branch or bud to increase bushiness.

Herbaceous A plant with 'soft' small stems – annuals, perennials, ground covers – as opposed to woody plants with 'hard' stems, such as trees or shrubs. Also refers to evergreen shrubs that die down to the ground once a year, then grow back the next season.

Honeydew A shiny, sticky substance, secreted by aphids and scale, found on the leaves on which they are feeding. It attracts ants and certain fungi.

Horticultural variety see **Plant Classification.**

Humus Soft brown or black material formed by the decomposition of animal or vegetable matter. In common landscape use, it is semi-decomposed plant matter – leaves, twigs, grass clippings, or sawdust used as a mulch or soil improvement.

Hybrid see **Plant classification**.

L

Lath When used in reference to gardens or nurseries, means any overhead structure that provides shade or frost protection.

Layering A method of propagation, either in the ground or 'air layering' on branches, in which roots are encouraged to form at a cut in the stem.

Leaching The process of watering the soil to saturation so that the water percolating down through the soil will carry with it unwanted salts to a depth beyond the roots.

Leaflets see **Bipinnate**.

M

Mulch Loose material, such as ground bark, peat moss, pebble bark, or gravel, placed over the soil in a thin layer as a protective element. It serves to slow down evaporation, prevent weed seeds from reaching the soil, insulate the soil against extreme temperatures, or to improve appearance.

N

Node A joint where a branch forms or a leaf starts to grow.

O

Offsets ('Pups') A method some plants use to reproduce themselves, by new plants growing out of the base of the mother plant. Date palms are a good example. The offset, or pup, can be transplanted by driving a shovel or other sharp instrument down between the plants, so that part of the root system is attached to the offset when it is lifted out of the ground.

Organic matter In gardening usage, refers to ground bark, humus, peat moss, or manure, used to improve the soil.

P

Perennial Technically, a plant that lives more than two years. In common usage, a small herbaceous shrub that may or may not die back during the winter.

Perlite A mineral expanded by heat, to form small, white, absorbent kernels. Used in the soil medium for propagating cuttings, and sometimes for lightweight soils. Also an insulating material.

Petal A modified leaf, usually coloured, which forms part of a flower.

Pinching back A method by which lateral growth is encouraged on a plant by removing the leading bud or buds.

Pinnate A type of leaf structure where leaves form directly off a stem.

Pistil The female, stalk-like part of a flower, usually found at its centre. The recipient of pollen.

Plant classification The botanical order in which plants are classified by similarities and requirements.
Family: The broad classification in which similarities of seed production, leaf shape, fruit type, and growth habit are categorized. The Latin family name is not included in the plant's botanical name. Example: *Ficus retusa nitida* is in the *Moraceae* family.
Genus: A plant family is divided into genera (plural of genus) in which each plant has more closely related characteristics. *Ficus* is the genus name *Ficus retusa nitida*. The first letter in a genus name is capitalized.
Species: A further subdivision with closer characteristics. *Retusa* is the species name in *Ficus retusa nitida*. The first letter is not capitalized.
Variety: Infrequently a third word in a botanical name will show a sub-species, thus *Ficus retusa nitida*.
Horticultural variety: Varieties that have been developed in nurseries to produce a particular flower colour, or leaf shape, or disease resistance. Accepted usage is for the named variety of a species to be within quotation marks. Example: *Nerium oleander* 'Petite Salmon'.
Hybrid: The result of crossing two species, varieties or strains.
Strain: Plants whose characteristics are slightly different from another plant, but not enough to merit a separate classification. Referred to more often in agricultural plants, such as a salt-tolerant strain of wheat.

Pollination The process of fertilization of plants by the transfer of pollen from the male portion of a flower (stamen) to the female portion (pistil). Some plants have both male and female parts on the same flower, and the transfer takes place by wind action causing the two parts to rub together. On other species, wind, bees, or other insects will transfer the pollen from a male plant to a female plant. In extreme cases, such as the date palm, this transfer may need to be made by man to ensure success. Following fertilization, fruit or seeds are developed.
    Some fruit trees, such as citrus, are self-pollinating, but most deciduous fruit trees

need another tree or another variety of tree to act as a pollinator.

R

Rhizome A thickened underground stem that grows laterally by creeping through the soil. Bamboo and iris are examples.

Rootbound The condition where a plant has been in its container too long, and fleshy white roots have girdled the root ball. When planting rootbound plants carefully scrape or prise the matted roots away from the soil with a thumb or knife. If this is not done, the plant may never grow larger than its present size, due to constriction of the roots.

Rosette A circular cluster of overlapping leaves.

Rust A type of fungus that infects leaves, and is evident by colonies of minute, yellow or tan spores on the leaf.

S

Salinity Excess salts in the soil, generally caused by frequent light waterings with water that is high in salts. Can be avoided by infrequent, heavy waterings, and periodically leaching the salts from the soil by saturation. Salinity is evident by leaf edges yellowing or browning. It can stunt plant growth.

Segment In some plants (such as tulips and daffodils), the sepal and petal form one structure, called a 'segment'.

Sepal Modified leaves (usually green) which protect the flower in bud. In some cases they are fused together and called the 'calyx'.

Single flowers A flower with the normal configuration of slightly overlapping petals.

Species see **Plant classification**.

Sphagnum Type of moss from bogs. Most peat moss is a form of decomposed sphagnum. You can buy bags of sphagnum moss, which is used in planting wire baskets or in propagating by air layering.

Spore A primitive type of cell which has the ability to reproduce new plants. Ferns, algae, and moss are grown from spores.

Stamen The male reproductive organ of a flower.

Standard Common usage now means a tree grown with a single trunk, with branching starting at approximately 1.8m (6ft). Most street trees are standards, to enable pedestrians and cars to pass under the foliage. Also refers to a plant whose natural spreading growth habit has been pruned and trained as a single trunk. Tree roses are an example.

Stolon A creeping stem that runs laterally, rooting into the ground at intervals from nodes. Bermuda grass spreads by means of stolons.

Strain see **Plant classification**.

Sucker growth Unwanted shoots that appear on the lower part of tree trunks, large branches, or out of the ground. Most plants that you are pruning to keep a clean trunk will, after two or three prunings, no longer produce this lower growth. Two notorious exceptions to this rule are oleanders and olive trees.

Systemic A substance that is introduced into a plant's system, generally through the roots, such as systemic insecticides and weed killers.

T

Taproot A single, large, fleshy root that grows straight down into the soil. The best known example is probably the carrot. However, in arid climates, many trees and shrubs send down very deep taproots in their search for water.

Tender Sensitive to frost or cold weather.

Tendril A string-like curling projection on some vines and other climbers that enables them to cling to trellises or other supports.

Thinning out Pruning out branches to thin, or open up, the interior of a plant. Also refers to removing newly grown seedlings to thin them out to the recommended spacing.

Topiary A pruning technique whereby compact-growing plants are trained into exotic geometric or animal shapes.

Tuber Thickened, underground, stem-like bulbs and corms, similar to rhizomes. Tuberous begonias are an example, but the most famous tuber is the potato.

V

Variety see **Plant classification**.

Vermiculite A mineral (Mica) that is expanded by heat to form brownish-tan kernels, used in lightweight soils or as a propagating medium.

W

Wettable powder A finely ground pesticide that can be mixed with water, and sprayed on plants, or on the ground as a soil drench.

Whorls A number of leaves, stems, or flowers, growing in a circular pattern from a single node or joint on a branch.

INDEX

Illustration references are given in
bold type

141